The Clash of Emp

by

Neil E. Allison BA BD MPhil LGSM DipESB CF

Photo] [Wakefield.

REV. E. L. WATSON, C.F.

First Edition: Published by the United Navy, Army and Air Force Board 2008

Acknowledgements

I have been working on the Official History of the United Navy, Army and Air Force Board for a few years now but, as a serving military chaplain have suffered serious interruptions to this work when deployed on operations. If it was not for my vast army of helpers I could not have completed this important work. My sincere thanks to all who helped with my research for this history, especially Susan Mills, Librarian/Archivist at Regent's Park College who not only gave good advice but spent a great deal of time photocopying on my behalf; David Powell, Senior Special Cataloguer at Dr Williams Library who did so much digging on my behalf; Alan Robinson who generously shared information gained in his Ph.D research; and Peter Howson who helped with information concerning the deaths of WWI chaplains. Also Mark Offord who photocopied the personnel files of Military Chaplains, and Graham White and David Stowe who helped locate and copy out files. Eleanor Rance who shared her discoveries concerning R.A.F chaplaincy, and Bethany Allison, my daughter, who scanned numerous photographs some of which appear in this book. The late John Murray; then Secretary of the United Navy, Army and Air Force Board, who allowed me to access U.B. files; Ian McFarlane, who took over responsibility from John Murray; and Jonathan Woodhouse, the Deputy Chaplain General, for their enthusiastic support and encouragement. David Blake, Curator of the RAChD Museum, who was a constant source of practical help and encouragement and Ieun Elfryn Jones who located and offered translation of Welsh articles. Thanks also to William Speirs who was interviewed and Alisdair Nicol who did the interviewing; Brian Talbot, the series editor, who helped me locate relevant books and was a constant source of encouragement; and to Ruth Allison, my wife, who was a constant source of ideas and helped with the research for this series.

PREFACE

I am honoured to be able to write this foreword for the first volume of the Official History of the United Board. Neil Allison, as our official historian, has begun a daunting single handed work to chronicle the activities and history of the United Board in its various incarnations since 1914. He is to be highly commended for rising to the challenge of producing this much needed work. The United Board is indebted to him for all that he has done to preserve the precious record of the work of our chaplains both in this volume and the two subsequent ones which will bring us up to the present day.

Writing now for a volume that begins with one war and ends with another is a reminder that we are never far from conflict as is the case currently. It highlights the fact that chaplains play an invaluable role in peace time, but I dare to suggest are even more beneficial in times of war and conflict.

It is humbling to read of the exploits of the many gifted and Godly chaplains who served during the period of this volume of the history and to recognise that some inevitably lost their lives in the service of Christ and their fellow service personnel. The United Board has sometimes been seen as the Cinderella grouping of chaplains because of the fewer numbers. It should be clear to anyone reading this part of the history that such a description is certainly not deserved in any particular. The constituent denominations can be justly proud of the role that their chaplains have played in the 1914 – 1939 period.

In my role as Secretary to the United Navy Army and Air force Board, I have the opportunity to meet with and support the current group of chaplains that come under our denominational oversight. We are again in a situation where war and conflict predominates and our chaplains – both men and women – are at the forefront of service life, serving with immense dedication, spiritual depth, compassion and strength of character. I wholeheartedly commend this work to you and pray that you will find it challenging and a cause for thanksgiving to God for those who have served the King and the Kingdom.

Ian M McFarlane
Secretary of the United Board
Great Bookham

June 2008

FOREWORD

Capturing the history of the unique ministry offered by United Board chaplains within the Royal Navy, Army and Royal Force is a daunting task and long overdue. The challenge has been more than met in this outstanding first volume, 'The Clash of Empires 1914-1939.' Here, Neil Allison sets out both the genesis of the United Board, traditionally understood as the 9th October 1914 when, 'the first two U.B. chaplains were commissioned and sent to France', and the years of Peace and Remembrance before the dark prospect of a Second World War cast its shadow over Europe in 1939.

The excellent use of Primary and Secondary sources establishes the scholarly credentials of the book but this is combined with both brightly sparkling and deeply moving personal stories of United Board chaplains ministering in the name of Christ on the battle fields of The First World War. This is underlined by the Army Chaplains' Department being honoured for its war-time work by being given the 'Royal' title and so becoming the Royal Army Chaplains' Department.

Neil Allison clearly describes the ecclesiastical and political background to the formation of the 'United Navy and Army Board' through to the United Board involvement in helping to establish the newly forming RAF Chaplaincy Service in 1918 to which several Army chaplains serving with the Royal Flying Corps were transferred.

Histories come in all shapes and sized, emphases and acknowledgements. This first of three volumes focuses more strongly on the story of United Board Army Chaplains but volumes two and three give greater weight to Royal Navy and Royal Air Force United Board chaplains. Taken together the three volumes bring strong scholarship and spirituality to the story of the Ministry and Mission of United Board chaplains from all three Armed Services. I am delighted to commend this 'labour of love' in the hope that readers may draw vision and inspiration from the exploits of our forebears.

The Reverend Jonathan Woodhouse QHC BA BSc MTh CF(UB)
Deputy Chaplain-General
Royal Army Chaplains' Department
Upavon

September 2008

DEDICATED TO THE MEMORY OF

Ash, John	United Methodist	1917
Ashton, F. W.	United Methodist	1918
Bray, Albert	Baptist	1924
Burns, Joseph D.	Congregationalist	1918
Edwards, Evan	Congregationalist	1918
Fraser, Donald	Baptist	1918
Hardy, J. H.	Congregationalist	1918
Heading, W. H.	Baptist	1918
Horton, Paul F.	Moravian	1917
Howell, T.	Congregationalist	1917
Jones, W. E.	Baptist	1918
Onslow-Carleton, William	Congregationalist	1918
Powley, Walter	Salvation Army	1918
Raine, F.	United Methodist	1918
Tomkins, W. H.	Baptist	1918
Veryard, A. T.	Baptist	1917
Wood, H. W.	Baptist	1918

Contents

List of Abbreviations

A.Ch.D.	Army Chaplains' Department
A.C.G.	Assistant Chaplain General
B.B.C.	British Broadcasting Corporation
B.E.F.	British Expeditionary Force
B.T.	Baptist Times and Freeman
B.Q.	Baptist Quarterly
B.U.G.B.I.	Baptist Union of Great Britain and Ireland
C.B.	Commander Bath
C.G.	Chaplain General
C.F.	Chaplain to the Forces
C.F.(U.B.)	United Board Chaplain to the Forces
C.O.	Conscientious Objector
Cong.	Congregational Union of England and Wales
C.W.	Christian World
D.S.O.	Distinguished Service Order
A.I.C.	Interdenominational Advisory Committee
M.C.	Military Cross
M.I.D.	Mention in Dispatches
O.B.E.	Order of the British Empire
O.C.F.	Officiating Chaplain to the Forces
P.M.	Primitive Methodist
P.O.W.	Prisoner of War
P.R.C.C.	Principal Roman Catholic Chaplain
R.A.Ch.D.	Royal Army Chaplains' Department
R.A.F.	Royal Air Force
R.N.	Royal Navy
S.A.	Salvation Army
S.B.M.	Scottish Baptist Magazine
W.O.	War Office
U.B.	United Navy and Army Board / post 1918 United Navy, Army & Air Force Board
U.M.	United Methodist

Chapter One: Introduction

Spiritual leaders have had a long history of service with the armed forces even before the concept of chaplain existed. From the time of Joshua[1] in the Old Testament spiritual leaders have been actively involved with the military. Centuries later Christian clerics deployed with their forces as combatants often leading their own armies. In 1350 clerics began to be deployed more formally as chaplains, their role increasingly becoming focussed on the spiritual and less on that of the combatant.

It was during the time of the English Civil War (1642-1645)[2] that ministers dissenting from the established church had their first opportunity to serve as military chaplains with the forces of Parliament to defend the 'Crown Rights' of King Jesus. Many of these dissenters[3] were Baptist and Congregationalist. Oliver Cromwell's New Model Army and Navy had created a New Model chaplaincy service to serve it effectively and this was long before the advent of the Army Chaplains Department (A.Ch.D.) which would not be organized until 1796. Dissenting chaplains served under the leadership of a Presbyterian, Master Bowles and an Independent, Master Hugh Peters. Although very little is known about these two, we do know that this chaplains' service was well organised and may well have been the inspiration behind the creation of the A.Ch.D. in 1796.[4] Understandably after the return of the monarchy under Charles II (1630-1685) these dissenters, whose independence demonstrated their unwillingness to be controlled by the state, were viewed with suspicion by the government and its forces and thus fell from grace. It was not until 1796 that dissenters were formally allowed to serve in the forces, on condition they were to attend services provided by the Anglican chaplains and had to register themselves using the general term of 'Protestant.' They also had to declare that they had no 'rupture' with the State.[5] In the same year on the 23rd of September the A.Ch.D. was formed under the forceful leadership of John Gamble, the first Chaplain General. It was formed to

---

[1] Joshua 6

[2] For a detailed introduction see Anne Lawrence, *Parliamentary Army Chaplains 1642-1651.* (Woodbridge: Boydell Press, 1990) See also Neil E. Allison, 'Baptist Military Chaplaincy during the Great War 1914-1918,' Unpublished M.Phil. Thesis, University of Wales, 2006, pp.37-41

[3] The term 'Dissenter' is used to describe Baptist and Congregationalists until 1914. Thereafter the term 'Free Church' is used to denote these denominations, together with some other Protestant Non-Conformists following the new more constructive relationship with the British State.

[4] Allison, 'Baptist Military Chaplaincy,' p.38

[5] For a detailed introduction see Michael Snape, *The Redcoat and Religion: The Forgotten History of the British Soldier from the Age of Marlborough to the Eve of the First World War*, (London: Routledge, 2005) See Allison, 'Baptist Military Chaplaincy,' pp.43-48

provide effective Anglican chaplains for the army and deal with the corruption that dominated chaplaincy provision. Walter T. Steven wrote that these reforms were inspired by "The moral, spiritual and social awakening under John Wesley and his friends that was shaking the Britain of those days, and out of which many reforms grew."[6] In spite of these reforms it was not until 1839 that dissenters were eventually allowed to attend services in their own tradition. However, few dissenting ministers were able to get access to lead these services and therefore, for the majority, this new religious freedom was little more than theoretical. It was not until 1903 that Free Church soldiers could attest their denominational allegiance openly on their personal records and have their religious needs officially met.

The greatest breakthrough for dissenters in the military came about as a result of the Great War (1914-1918). The government needed to recruit more soldiers and chaplains to serve them. Many recruits and potential recruits came from the industrial North of England and Wales where the Free Churches dominated. The War Office wanted soldiers and the leaders of the Free Churches wanted complete recognition for their ministers as chaplains. The War Office was in no position to call the shots. Two months after war was declared, Baptist, Congregational, Primitive and United Methodists were able to serve as commissioned army chaplains. The Royal Navy, who needed far less chaplains, finally accepted them as commissioned chaplains in 1916 but did not allow them to go to sea until after the war was over in 1920. Therefore this volume will concentrate on U.B. Chaplains serving in the British army.

The commissioning of these chaplains was only made possible when Baptists joined together with Congregationalists, Primitive Methodists and United Methodists to create the United Congress (U.C.) in 1914. Within a few months this Congress developed into the United Navy and Army Board (U.B.) although it tended to be viewed by the War Office as one unified denomination. This is the official story of this United Navy, Army and Air Force Board and those that served within it as chaplains from 1914 until 1939 when Britain was again drawn into another devastating war.

This is not an uncritical history; the chaplains were a product of their age and an understanding of the cultural context of the time is essential. Therefore some time is given to the national and religious climate in which the U.B. was created and served. Nonetheless the story of the U.B. and its chaplains during the Great War is an inspiring one. These chaplains served effectively in the crucible of war and for

---

[6] Walter T. Steven, *In this Sign*, (Toronto: The Ryerson Press, 1948), p.2

many their work was marked by outward success and even revival. Some U.B. chaplains, influenced by the 1905 Welsh revival, continued to see the power of the Spirit working amongst the troops behind the lines. Always the focal point of their ministry was Christ and God's offer, through him, of reconciliation between a fallen and broken humanity and a holy, but embracing God.

The foundation for this particular volume was my 2006 M.Phil thesis entitled "Baptist Military Chaplaincy during the Great War (1914-1918)." Obviously a lot has been cut away and re-written. The work of the other denominations represented in the U.B. has been expanded and more detail given. However, it must be recognised that Baptists dominated the U.B. at this time. The Organisational Secretary, J.H. Shakespeare, was a Baptist as was Aubrey who followed him. Therefore the key representative on the A.I.C. was a Baptist, but with responsibility to faithfully represent the other denominations of the U.B. The reader will also notice that the revivalism experienced at the Front was primarily a Baptist experience although not exclusively. This was for two reasons. Firstly, revivalism was a part of Baptist self understanding and practice and secondly, they were able self promoters and occasionally this was a point of tension within the U.B. Therefore, on occasion, some imbalance will be present. However, I have attempted to represent all the U.B. denominations while treating the U.B. as a corporate denominational body which is how they were perceived within A.Ch.D and military circles.

Chapter Two: In the Beginning

I. Denominations of the United Board

Although the U.B. tended to be generally thought of as a single denomination by the War Office, it was actually formed from various groups with very different cultures and histories. The founding denominations of the U.B. were Baptist, Congregationalist, United and Primitive Methodist.

a. Baptist

Baptists in general have been opposed to the concept of a centralized denomination. They would rather see themselves as a group of autonomous congregations that have chosen to affiliate themselves together in a Union of churches. The Baptist Union began its life in 1813 bringing together Calvinist Baptist pastors and congregations that had already recognised the benefits of membership in regional associations of churches. In 1832 this Union reorganised and redefined itself to bring together those Baptist churches and ministers who could "agree in the sentiments usually denominated evangelical."[7] This would allow for a more positive relationship with the New Connexion General Baptists, who were Arminian in theology. In 1873 the Baptist Union continued with the key term evangelical and stated a 'Declaration of Principle.' It stated that "in this Union it is fully recognized that every separate church has liberty to interpret and administer the laws of Christ, and that the immersion of believers is the only Christian baptism."[8] In 1891 the New Connexion General Baptists merged with the Baptist Union and formed the Baptist Union of Great Britain and Ireland. In 1904 they declared that basis of Union was the belief:

1. That the Lord Jesus Christ is the sole and absolute authority in all matters pertaining to faith and practice, as revealed in the Holy Scriptures, and that each Church has liberty to interpret and administer His Laws.

2. That Christian Baptism is the immersion in water into the Name of the Father, Son and the Holy Ghost, of those who have professed repentance towards God and faith in our Lord Jesus Christ who 'died for our sins according to the Scriptures; was buried, and rose again the third day.'

3. That it is the duty of every disciple to bear personal witness to the Gospel of

---

[7] Cited by Ernest A. Payne, *The Baptist Union a Short History*, (London: The Carey Press Limited, 1959), pp.3-4

[8] Cited by Payne, *Short History*, p.4

Jesus Christ, and to take part in the evangelisation of the world.[9]

In 1906 "our God and Saviour" was added to the first clause and this was the basis of Principle that was extant when the Baptist Union was accepted as a 'Sending Church'[10] by the War Office.

J. H. Shakespeare, who was to become the first Organising Secretary of the U.B., was beginning to gain prominence during this period. In the 1892 Spring Assembly he challenged the delegates that the Baptist Union needed better denominational organisation in order to maximise their evangelistic work. He proclaimed:

> Unorganised Congregationalism is today only another name for selfishness... God forgive us that we have been in the midst of the perishing multitudes, not like the compassionate Master, but enjoying our religious privileges, rapt in glorious memories and clutching at a dead idol, the brazen and deceptive serpent of an extreme and selfish independency.[11]

Shakespeare became the Baptist Union Secretary in 1898, and would remain in that office until 1925. At the turn of the century "Evangelism, organisation and social acceptance were...(the) central issues in Baptist church life as the new century dawned"[12] For Shakespeare the Baptist denomination was "the greatest Protestant evangelical community on earth."[13] The Baptist Union of Great Britain and Ireland would supply one hundred and one chaplains for military service from 1914.

b. Congregationalist

R. Tudor Jones wrote that "'The Congregationalist way' emerged as a distinctive and powerful expression of the Christian faith in England and Wales in the tempestuous years that followed 1640 but its pre-history extends back over the previous ninety years."[14] Like the Baptists, the Congregationalists' first experience

---

[9] Cited by Payne, *Short History*, p.5

[10] 'Sending Church' is used to denote any denomination that is recognized by the War Office and is able to supply chaplains to the military for commissioning.

[11] *Baptist Church Extension in Large Towns* A paper presented to the B.U.G.B.I. Assembly 1892. Cited by Payne, *Short History*, p.337

[12] Cited by Payne, *Short History*, p.338

[13] Ian M. Randall, *The English Baptists of the 20th Century*, (Didcot: The Baptist Historical Society 2005), p.50

[14] R. Tudor Jones, *Congregationalism in England 1662-1962*, (London: Independent Press Ltd 1962), p.13

of formal military chaplaincy occurred during the English Civil War. Oliver Cromwell himself was a Congregationalist. In October 1871 the Congregational Union was formed under the leadership of Alexander Hannay with a more centralised government which resulted in greater efficiency for this new denomination.[15] These and later changes were thought to have inspired the centralising reforms of the Baptist Union led by Shakespeare. However, by 1900 Congregationalism found itself face-to-face with several difficult theological and intellectual questions. Biblical criticism had been accepted by the majority of the intellectual leaders of the denomination and a Liberal Modernist theology was following in its wake and many of the younger ministers and laymen found it more satisfying than the theology of their fathers.[16]

Experience rather than doctrine became the key guiding factor within this new Congregationalism with the exaltation of "morality and social action."[17] The end result, as Tudor Jones concluded, was a "peculiar brand of orthodoxy in which Modernistic elements together with the Social Gospel were tempered by some measure of adherence to the traditional Evangelical formulae."[18] When war broke out in 1914 the Congregational Union joined with the other recognised denominations that were to form the United Board and supplied one hundred chaplains for the Front.

c. Primitive Methodist

The Primitive Methodist denomination began its life on May 30th 1811 when the Camp Meeting Methodists and the Clowesites came together to form one administrative body.[19] They "sought to propagate what they deemed to be primitive Methodism."[20] In 1843 the denomination expanded materially with the building of many new buildings and consolidated its position within the nation's life.[21] Mission work that had been important since the denomination's foundation, developed beyond the British Isles into the nations under the influence or control of the British Empire.[22] It is not surprising that this evangelically vibrant denomination would see, as with the other Free Churches, an opportunity to gain

---

[15] Ibid, pp.312-313
[16] Ibid, p.347
[17] Ibid, p.347
[18] Ibid, p.354
[19] Kendall, *The Origin and History of the Primitive Methodist Church, Volume One*, (London: Edwin Alton, 1906), p.117
[20] Ibid, p.116
[21] Kendall, *The Origin and History of the Primitive Methodist Church, Volume Two*, (London: Edwin Alton, 1906), p.455
[22] Ibid, p.481

recognition and reach men with the gospel. In 1914 they set up a Board to oversee the denomination's work in the military. Therefore, when the war broke out Primitive Methodists were well organised and able to respond effectively to Shakespeare's invitation to join the 'Round Table Talks' that were to lay the foundation of the United Board. After the war the Primitive Methodist Church united with the Wesleyans on the 20th September 1932 and left the U.B.

d. United Methodists

The United Methodist church was a very young but influential denomination by the beginning of the war in 1914. As a formal denomination it came into being on the 10th September 1907. The United Methodist Church was created by uniting the Methodist New Connection; the Bible Christian Methodists and the United Methodist Free Church.[23] "All three stood for the same two ideals, first, for the integrity of Methodist Doctrine... and second, for democratic or representative Government as opposed to the autocratic or oligarchic system to which Wesleyans for a long time clung most tenaciously."[24] The unity was also based on a common Arminian doctrinal statement placing the Bible as containing "a revelation of the will of God to man, and furnish a sufficient rule of faith and practice" and placing particular emphasis on the finished work of Christ and justification by faith leading to the new birth. This doctrinal statement also placed an implicit emphasis on the need for mission. It stated that "God wills not the death of any sinner, but requires repentance towards Himself and faith in our Lord Jesus Christ as necessary to salvation."[25] By 1913 this new evangelical denomination turned its attention to the Navy and Army and sought to gain recognition from the military authorities which would enable them to supply United Methodist chaplains. This application for recognition was rejected by the authorities on the grounds that they had insufficient numbers serving in both services to warrant chaplains. The war changed all this and large numbers of United Methodists joined the ranks of the military. A conservative estimate puts the number serving in the forces at 80,000.[26] "This occasioned so much concern on the part of mothers and fathers about the spiritual care of these boys under the new and perilous conditions of war that the Connexional Committee gladly accepted the invitation of the Baptists and Congregationalists to join them along with the Primitive Methodists to constitute the four Churches into the United Board, with Chaplains set apart for the care of the adherents of all four Churches during the period of the war."[27] In total forty

[23] *The Story of the United Methodist Church*, (London: Henry Hooks, 1932), p.1
[24] Ibid, p.1
[25] Ibid, p.23
[26] Ibid, p.33
[27] Ibid, p.32

two United Methodist chaplains would serve during the war. The first of these was Joseph Wallett who was commissioned in 1915. As a denomination they were well suited to chaplaincy service as can be seen by the awards listed in Appendix One. J. Penry Davey was appointed 'Assistant Principal Chaplain to the United Board' with the relative rank of Brigadier General.[28] After the war the United Methodist Church united with the Wesleyans on the 20th September 1932 leaving a short, but outstanding, history.

e. The United Board an Ecumenical Model

R. Tudor Jones explains why, in his view, these various denominations were able to work together as a United Board to such a degree that they were effectively seen as a single denomination. He wrote:

> By the middle of the nineteenth century, it was clear that the Nonconformist denominations had much in common. Differences could barely be discerned between Independents, Baptists, Methodists, Wesleyans and Unitarians in their chapels, their ecclesiastical organization, their services or the various societies which were established for their members It was clear that they all belonged to the same movement and, precisely because of this, they tended to make much of the often very trivial differences that did exist between them, and that gave rise to denominational jealousy. On the other hand, they formed a united front in their attitude towards public and national questions.[29]

In my view the four denominations which made up the U.B. were able to join together because of their common desire to gain official recognition by the military in order to gain prestige and perhaps more importantly, their desire to evangelise the masses. Certainly the U.B. was willing to extend its boundaries by accepting a Moravian chaplain and, grudgingly, administrative responsibility for five Salvation Army chaplains. The U.B. was unwilling to accept the Salvation Army as a constituted church, viewing it rather as a para-church organisation predominantly because it did not celebrate the sacraments, but the War Office overruled the Board's concerns and insisted that it take responsibility for the Salvation Army chaplains. Unitarians were considered unorthodox by all the churches of the U.B. and were thus rejected outright when they applied for recognition.

---

[28] Ibid, p.119

[29] R. Tudor Jones, *Congregationalism in Wales*, (Cardiff: University of Wales Press 2004), p.198

II. The Foundation of the United Board

At the beginning of the First World War, the Liberal Government recognised the desperate need to recruit soldiers and sailors, and the Free Churches could offer this extra manpower in abundance. On the 10th November 1914 three thousand Free Churchmen packed into the City Temple in London to hear an address from the then Chancellor of the Exchequer David Lloyd George. Along with other Free Church speakers he encouraged the audience to get fully behind the war effort by joining up or supporting those that did. Although 60,000 Free Churchmen had already enlisted by this time,[30] it was necessary not only to recruit even more men but also to reassure the Free Churches that this was a holy war, a crusade in the defence of freedom. By using illustrations and language reminiscent of biblical tales, Lloyd George aroused sympathy and righteous outrage for Belgium by likening it to a victim, with Germany the bully and Britain the hero coming to the rescue. Lloyd George was a charismatic and clever speaker; he soon had his audience cheering as he assured them that they held the moral high ground and the "brave men who have died need not fear judgement, because it is our faith that 'sacrifice is ever the surest road to redemption.'[31] Randall perceptively explains that "Evangelicals, with their cross-centred theology, saw sacrifice as the way to victory."[32] Therefore "the message of the cross was turned into one of national self-preservation."[33] This can be clearly illustrated by G. E. Minnear C.F. (U.B.) who developed his theology during the first Somme Offensive in 1916. He wrote "[t]hey died valiantly in the name of Righteousness. It is probable that in life they were not all saints. But such a death for such a cause reflects a touch of nobleness; places them in the ranks of a long line of honoured martyrs, and links them on to Calvary."[34] It seems that this belief began to arise from the chaplains' experience of the trauma of war and the 'self sacrificing' nature of the British Tommy caught up within it. It was just impossible for these evangelical chaplains to believe that such 'nobleness' could be in such abundant evidence if they were not Christian.

What really caught the imagination of the Free Churchmen was the spirit of Cromwell - the idea of a godly army fighting for a just cause against tyranny. The 11th September 1914 edition of the *Baptist Times* encouraged its readers to "(j)oin the armies that are fighting for the Kingdom of God as surely did the Puritans in

---

[30] Alan Wilkinson, *Dissent or Conform? War, Peace and the English Churches 1900-1945*, (London: SCM 1986), p.26

[31] Ibid, p.26

[32] Ian M. Randall, 'The Role of Conscientious Objectors. British Evangelicals and the Great War' (*Anabaptism Today*, February 1996) p.12

[33] Kenneth D. Brown, *A Social History of the Nonconformist Ministry in England and Wales 1800-1930*, (Oxford: Clarendon Press, 1988), p.233

[34] Henry Smith, *Stories from the Front by United Methodist Chaplains*, (London: Henry Hooks 1917), p.18

Cromwell's day."[35] In fact "the invocation of Cromwell in support of the war effort became a common occurrence among leading Nonconformists, which was a new slant as hitherto he had hardly been seen as a supporter of the voluntary principle."[36] This spirit was further encouraged with the re-printing of Cromwell's *Soldier's Catechism*. Even a Primitive Methodist chaplain was delighted to have a Batman appointed to him by the name of Cromwell.[37]

The Free Churchmen may have been manipulated by the politicians to support the war effort, but certain Free Church leaders also grasped that they could use their influence with these politicians to gain something positive for the Free Churches out of the war.[38] They saw the war as "both a challenge and an opportunity."[39] This is especially interesting because "these bodies entered on the war with very little of a chaplaincy tradition... nor did the Congregationalists or Baptists set up an Army Board when, from 1903 onwards, recognition and involvement in soldiers' matters was offered them by an organising War Office."[40] Robinson also concludes that the "expectation that the experience of war would turn soldiers towards God coincided with the national enthusiasm for the war and motivated the clergy to make strenuous recruiting efforts."[41] Their great hope was for a Christian revival and for formal State recognition. Shakespeare and R. J. Wells, a Congregationalist, as denominational Secretaries, saw an opportunity for further Free Church recognition and approached the War Office on the 14th August 1914 to request that Baptists and Congregationalists be recognised and appointed as commissioned chaplains. This was initially rejected by the War Office on 17th August 1914, although they did offer to appoint many more Officiating Chaplains to the Forces (O.C.F) i.e. civilian ministers who could care for the soldiers in barracks and the sailors working in the docks. Although this was a step in the right direction, it did not satisfy Shakespeare and Wells who were concerned about those Free Churchmen sent abroad out of reach of its O.C.F.s. Shakespeare, therefore, went to Parliament and approached David Lloyd George, and the Chief

---

[35] Wilkinson, *Dissent or Conform?*, p.48

[36] Ruston, 'Protestant Nonconformist,' p.247

[37] Phil J. Fisher, *Khaki Vignettes*, (London: Joseph Johnson 1917), p. 51

[38] Michael Townsend, 'John Howard Shakespeare: Prophet of Ecumenism,' *BQ*, Vol.37, No.6, April 1998, p.300

[39] Alan Ruston, 'Protestant Nonconformist Attitudes towards the First World War,' Ed: Alan P. F Sell and Anthony R. Cross, *Protestant Nonconformity in the Twentieth Century*, (Carlisle: Paternoster Press 2003), p.246

[40] Ronald Thomson, *Ministering to the Forces The Story of the Baptist and Congregational Chaplains and the work of the United Navy, Army and Air Force Board 1914-1964*, (B.U.G.B.I. & C.U. of England &Wales. Sussex, 1964), pp.284-285

[41] Alan Charles Robinson, 'The Role of British Army Chaplains during World War Two,' Unpublished Ph.D Thesis University of Liverpool December 1999, p.22

Whip of the Liberal Party, Mr. Percy Illingworth, who were both Baptists.[42] There was also a growing desire for such recognition within the pages of the *Christian World*[43] a prominent Free Church Newspaper. After negotiations the government and Lord Kitchener promised that the rights of Baptists and Congregationalists would be as "scrupulously protected" as those of other denominations.[44] Shakespeare and Wells were obviously encouraged by these promises but it still did not give the official recognition they desired. In November 1914 Shakespeare, no doubt because he needed to strengthen his case for Free Church recognition within the forces, invited representatives[45] of the Primitive Methodists and the United Methodists to attend a 'Round Table Conference.'[46] The Primitive and United Methodists had not been inactive in working towards their own recognition. As early as 1913 the United Methodists attempted to gain recognition and commissioned chaplains with the War Office but were refused because of lack of numbers.[47] The Primitive Methodists had also been pro-active and had set up a 'Board' to oversee 'Army Work' in September 1914 under the leadership of George Standing[48] who would serve as a United Board chaplain. One of its first acts was to object "to their men being put down as Wesleyans and sought their own column in the army returns after 'Congregational or Baptist.'"[49] At this meeting the "scheme of co-operation by the four denominations in Navy and Army work then submitted by Mr Shakespeare and Mr Wells was approved by the authorities in each of the denominations."[50] This development in wider Free Church representation within the United Board was to win the day and gained formal recognition within the military.

On the 11th November 1914 a conference between Free Church leaders was held in London and had representatives from the Baptist Union of Great Britain and Ireland; the Congregational Union of England and Wales; Primitive Methodists; United Methodists and the Welsh Calvinistic Methodists. The Calvinistic Methodists at this meeting reported that they had discovered that "as a matter of practice that their Welsh speaking men were put down... as Wesleyans and their English speaking men were allotted to the Presbyterians and that as a matter of fact the Government recognised them as Presbyterians and classified them as

---

[42] See Douglas C. Sparkes 'Percy Holden Illingworth and the Last Liberal Government,' *BQ*, Vol.39, No.7, July 2002

[43] Ralph Blake, 'Free Church Federation,' *Christian World*, 10th September 1914

[44] Thomson, *Ministering*, p.8

[45] Andrew Crombie, Henry Hooks and Henry Smith

[46] Smith, *Stories from the Front*, p.10; See also *The Story of the United Methodist Church*, p.117

[47] Thompson, 'Free Church Army Chaplain,' p.296

[48] Ibid, p.296

[49] Ibid, p.296

[50] Smith, *Stories from the Front by United Methodist Chaplains*, p.10

such."[51] With this in mind they determined "to refer the question to their own Committee with a view to ascertaining whether they would prefer to strengthen their position with the Presbyterians or to come in with us."[52] They did not meet with the Board again because they had decided to gain recognition directly from the military authorities.[53] The Welsh Calvinists had their first chaplain commissioned in 1914 with nine others following.[54] At this conference it was agreed to form a United Board to look after and promote Free Church interests within the Navy and Army. All correspondence related to this committee was left in the hands of Shakespeare and Wells. They met again on the 20th November 1914 and again on the 4th December 1914 "to consider the formation of a body representing the Nonconformist Churches, other than the Wesleyans and Presbyterians, to nominate chaplains and officiating clergymen and to deal with the War Office."[55] On the 14th January 1915[56] the United Navy and Army Board was formally established. The official U.B. Constitutional memoir, under the title of 'historical notes', stated that the U.B. was formed on the 9th October 1914 which is incorrect.[57] This was the date when E. L. Watson (Baptist) and J. J. L. Clayton (Congregationalist) were sent to France as part of the British Expeditionary Force under the auspices of the United Congress (U.C.). The work of the U.B. began through the U.C. before the U.B. was officially constituted, and was promulgated by the Baptist and Congregational denominational leadership, beginning on 14th August 1914 with their first approach to the War Office. The first annual meeting was held in October 1915. At this conference the gathering was informed that the U.B. represented four hundred and eighty O.C.F.s and eighty-four 'Temporary Chaplains.' Twenty-five of these were able to be present straight from the 'Front' to tell their stories.[58]

The U.B. was constituted in spite of opposition from Lord Kitchener, who referred to Baptists and Congregationalists as "superfluous and eccentric sects."[59] During Kitchener's conversations with Lloyd George, who supported the Nonconformist cause, he was reported as saying, "Come now, tell me the names of these sects for which you want Padres. Is this list right? Primitive Baptists, Calvinistic

---

[51] Thompson, The Free Church Army Chaplain , p.298
[52] Ibid, p.298
[53] Ibid, p.299
[54] Michael Snape, *The Royal Army Chaplains Department 1796-1953 Clergy under Fire*, (Woodbridge: Suffolk: Boydell Press, 2008), p. 201
[55] Thompson, The Free Church Army Chaplain, p.297
[56] Ibid, pp.297-299; See also Thomson, *Ministering to the Forces*, p.8; Robinson 'Role,' p.27
[57] *The Baptist Handbook 1935*, p.281
[58] 'Chaplains in Conference The Work of the United Army Board.' *BT*, October 29th 1915, p.704
[59] David Lloyd George, *War Memoirs of David Lloyd George Volume 1*, (London: Odhams Press Ltd), p.451. See also Robinson, 'Role,' p.23

Wesleyans, Congregational Methodists?"[60] One Baptist commentator noted: "It takes a lot of hammering to get a new idea into the head of a War Office, but Mr. Shakespeare is a good hand with the mallet, and supported by other Free Churchmen he has brought about a notable reformation." Shakespeare believed passionately that the "institution of the 'United Navy and Army Board' [would] be an important landmark in Free Church history."[61] Certainly, the creation of the U.B. enthused Free Churchmen with a new vision of what might be possible through its agency. J. C. Carlile believed that the U.B. "is a new creation, but it will revolutionise many things for the Free Church soldier,"[62] and George Kendall C.F. (U.B.) described it enthusiastically as a "heaven-sent blessing" and Shakespeare as "not only a genius for organisation, but the best friend a chaplain could ever have."[63] Certainly he was celebrated. George Standing sent a telegram to Shakespeare from the 'Front.' He wrote that "United Board Chaplains in the Field salute you. We hail your presidency as a token of the new day here."[64] Henry Smith C.F. (U.B.) simply and modestly recognised that "[t]he co-operation under the Board has been the closest and most cordial kind and has resulted in the work of caring for soldiers and sailors being done with an efficiency and thoroughness which would have been impossible if each denomination had acted separately."[65] Thompson concluded that "[t]he United Board came to be treated in practice as a separate and single denomination."[66]

The U.B. was initially created to represent the interests of Baptists, Congregationalists, United Methodists and Primitive Methodists within the Armed Forces and allowed recognised Ministers from these churches to officially serve as officiating and eventually, commissioned chaplains. The headquarters of this United Board was to be based at Baptist Church House, London, and its first Chairman was Shakespeare. He believed passionately that the formation of the U.B. had "a deep significance and (had) been swiftly followed by results of the most far reaching importance... It is the symbol that our churches are taking their part with resolution and sacrifice at this tremendous hour. In the cause of their country they will hold nothing back. They have accepted the responsibility for their soldier sons."[67] Peter Shepherd, in his authoritative history of the life of

---

[60] David Lloyd George, *Volume 1*, p.451

[61] N. Notewell, 'Impressions of Nicholas Notewell, Some Chaplains in Khaki' *BT* December 17th 1915 p.820

[62] J. C. Carlile, 'With the Troops at a Base in Northern France,' *BT*, March 19th 1915, p.183

[63] G. Kendall, 'Captain the Rev. E. L. Watson, C.F.,' *BT*, August 6th 1915, p.525. *BT* will be used for this publication in all future references.

[64] George Standing, 'Notes by the Way,' *The CW*, 3rd February 1916, p.3

[65] Smith, *Stories from the Front*, p.10

[66] Thompson, 'Free Church Chaplains,' p.300

[67] F. C. Spurr, *Some Chaplains in Khaki: An Account of the Work of Chaplains of the United Board*,

Shakespeare,[68] is convinced that the U.B. was ground-breaking because, firstly, it made an important contribution to the:

> attitudes about Free Church co-operation, and church unity in general. Secondly, it played a significant role in reflecting the fuller integration of Baptists, along with Nonconformity as a whole, into national life during the war. Thirdly, the existence of Baptist Ministers in the service of the Crown was an important step in the development of Baptist thinking about ministry.[69]

However not all Free Churchmen were as enthusiastic about the creation of the U.B. The Cambridge academic T. R. Glover saw little real significance in the creation of the U.B., which he viewed as "a dodge to let the War Office dispose of people it does *not* want to be bothered with. It has little other spiritual significance."[70] But, most were excited and supportive of this new Free Church venture into a Christian ministry nationally recognised and supported. The key aim of this U.B. was to assist in the recruiting of Chaplains for H. M. Forces and liaise with the appropriate Service authorities.

The original United Board members were:
J. H. Shakespeare B.U.G.B.I.[71]
Andrew Crombie U.M.
W. A. Hammond P.M.
Henry Hooks U.M.
Samual Horton P.M.[72]
John Mayles P.M.
George Standing P.M.
Henry Smith U.M.[73]
Richard J. Wells Cong.[74]

The challenge now faced was, would the U.B. live up to its own expectations and become a significant united Free Church body or simply become a useful administrative organisation to support the national war effort?

(London: Kingsgate 1916), p.7
[68] Peter Shepherd, *The Making of a Modern Denomination. John Howard Shakespeare and the English Baptists 1898-1924,*(Carlisle: Paternoster Press, 2001)
[69] Ibid, p.94
[70] Thompson, 'Free Church, ' p.301 Shakespeare writing to T. Tatlow 19th July 1915
[71] Denominational Secretary
[72] Denominational Secretary
[73] Denominational Secretary
[74] Denominational Secretary

III. The Work of the United Board

Once the U.B. was constituted it immediately appealed to the churches it represented for donations which would enable the creation of Christian Institutes and "Huts" for the soldiers' welfare, recreation and rest. To give a couple of examples, the Percy Illingworth Institute at Aldershot was supported by the Baptists, and the Cromwell Institute, also at Aldershot, was built by the Congregationalists and eight Huts were built by the Primitive Methodists.[75] Some of these Huts were simply initiated by individual United Board chaplains. Frank Fairfax C.F.(U.B.) who had found an unscathed annex of a college in France, made a placard with bold lettering outside the door declaring that this building was now the 'Free Church Institute.' Fairfax reflected that "[f]or a few glorious weeks the Free Churches of England had a citadel of their own in that town... the Institute gave us a recognised rendezvous, a more continuous opportunity, and a many-sided ministry."[76] Fortunately Fairfax described in some detail the outstanding work he accomplished in *Stories from the Front* in a 'few glorious weeks.'[77] This centre had a shop where cheap commodities could be bought. It had an 'Inner Room' where soldiers could relax and listen to a gramophone and play games, unless there was one who wanted to play the piano. There were also papers produced each evening. It was a place to find rest and it also gave amazing opportunities for chaplains to get to know their soldiers. Fairfax related a story when a young soldier crept into this room "with mud on his clothes and a dirty shrapnel helmet half hiding his features, stole to the piano and began lightly fingering the keys. Then he threw himself with abandon in the world of Rachmaninoff and Grieg, Tchaikovsky and Chopin, Dvorak and modern Russian composers... We saw more of him. Sometimes he played at our services. A Congregationalist, he was also a Bachelor of Science and as keenly devoted to chemistry as to music. And he was a private in this amazing army!"[78] This Hut also became a University and a place where the soldiers could meet with God. Fairfax said that "(t)here are times on active service when one may only preach for five minutes or less, but in our Institute on a Sunday night one could have complete attention for a full half hour. We had the gladness of seeing men decide to live a new life. A Salvationist came to me after a service and said he would devote himself afresh to God."[79] The Hut was also a place to try out new ideas.

One of our experiments was the Sunday night platform. The preacher was

[75] Thompson, 'Free Church Chaplain,' p.312
[76] Smith, *Stories from the Front*, p.67
[77] Ibid, p.67
[78] Ibid, p.70
[79] Ibid, pp.72-74

one of several leaders of worship. One night a lieutenant (a Wesleyan) took charge of the service, Private Foster Raine prayed, a Primitive Methodist read the lesson, my colleague made the announcements, a private (a Wesleyan) preached a sermon that men talked of for weeks. We continued that plan, which might be commended to our churches at home, as tending among other things to relieve the monotony of one man's personality dominating the services week after week. 'There are diversities of gifts, but the same Spirit.'[80]

During the Second World War John Macbeath shared his memories of working with soldiers in the 'Hut' environment when serving in the Great War as an army chaplain. He wrote that "I cherish the memory of many happy hours, great friendships, countless confidential chats; most hallowed of all were the occasions of Holy Communion, and the manifest conversion of some who became good soldiers of Jesus Christ..."[81]

The U.B. also encouraged the women of the churches, to make and collect 'comforts' for the troops on the front line. William Cramb Charteris C.F.(U.B.) described the kind of things that were sent: "Scarves, gloves, chocolates and most importantly cigarettes".[82] D. Merrick Walker O.C.F.(U.B.) while working as an officiating chaplain, before becoming the first U.B. commissioned Naval chaplain in 1916, described how he used such small comforts. He speaks of collecting and distributing "little comforts" at military centres and on Warships which were "the keys with which hearts and ears were opened to the gospel."[83] The U.B. also distributed, through its chaplains and institutes, "Daily papers, magazines, books, tracts, Gospels, and New Testaments. And the New Testaments [were] received more gladly than the rest."[84] Walker tells numerous stories of the spiritual interest of those serving within the forces, the tender joy of being able to share communion and how he was able to distribute 700 tracts on an army transport train. The urgency of this spiritual work is made very clear leaving no doubt in the readers' minds. He informs them: "(m)any of them have fallen since in the Dardenelles fighting. If the Saviour has gathered them to Himself our reward is complete."[85]

---

[80] Ibid, p.73

[81] John Macbeath, 'Scottish Baptist Churches Hut,' *SBM*, 75.7, July 1940, p.11

[82] Neil E. Allison, 'Shakespeare's Man at the Front,' *BQ*, Vol.41, No.4, October 2005, p.227

[83] D. Merrick Walker, 'The United Army Board. Serving the Soldiers and Sailors,' *SBM*, 41.8, August, 1915, p.118

[84] Ibid, p.118

[85] Ibid, p.119

The U.B. was very keen to promote its work and to continue to gain recognition for the Free Churches. They also used their published works to rejoice in their gospel ministry. The U.B.' s first written contribution to military chaplaincy was a *Memoranda of Information for Chaplains to the Forces and Officiating Clergymen of the United Navy and Army Board* published in 1916. This small brown booklet gave pragmatic advice on military etiquette and basic responsibilities, such as the newly posted chaplain calling to introduce himself to the Commanding Officer on arrival and leaving a visiting card in the Officers Mess when visiting different locations. It also gave advice on how to make arrangements for a Parade Service and who the correct person was to approach to make these arrangements. Naturally, this booklet stressed the importance of keeping accurate records of the men from their own denomination which would be helpful in arguing numbers with the War Office so as to gain more chaplains. Another aspect was to inform the chaplain of what he should expect to receive on commissioning, such as the payment of ten shillings a day. However, this booklet did not seek to define the role of the chaplain but stated that "A Chaplain's duties are very vaguely defined. As in the civilian ministry, most of his work is left to his own initiative. He must arrange Divine Services and classes of instruction; visit the Hospital and see any of his men who may be ill. In general terms, it is his duty to have regard to the material and religious welfare of his men."[86] This emphasis certainly gave encouragement for these chaplains to model their military ministry on their civilian one which, as will be seen, they tended to do.

The United Board's key contribution to Free Church chaplaincy history was *Some Chaplains in Khaki* which was published just after the first Somme offensive in 1916.[87] It was written by Frederic C. Spurr and the foreword was written by J. H. Shakespeare. This book gives a sanitised version of the war. This was a feature common in Victorian evangelistic literature. It was obviously written in order to gain support from the 'sending churches'[88] for their Evangelical Chaplains. It is shocking, to the modern reader, that *Chaplains in Khaki* could be written in such a style. Compare this record with Roman Catholic chaplain William Doyle's account which described moving forward during the Somme Offensive.
Doyle wrote that

[86] The United Board, *Memoranda of Information for Chaplains to the Forces and Officiating Clergymen of the United Navy and Army Board*, (1916), Section 6

[87] The Somme Offensive was the "main allied attack on the WESTERN FRONT in 1916. Launched on 1 July along a 30 km front running roughly north of the River Somme between Amiens and Peronne," eventually ending on the 18th November. This offensive gained 12 km of ground at the cost of 420,000 British casualties. See Pope & Wheal, *Dictionary of the First World War*, (Barnsley: Pen & Sword, 1995), pp.440-441

[88] 'The Sending Churches' is the term used for those denominations recognised by the Ministry of War as main line denominations who can supply chaplains for commissioning.

[t]he first part of our journey lay through a narrow trench, the floor of which consisted of deep thick mud, and the bodies of dead men trodden under foot. It was horrible beyond description, but there was no help for it, and on the half-rotten corpses of our own brave men we marched in silence, everyone busy with his own thoughts. I shall spare you gruesome details, but you can picture one's sensations as one felt the ground yield under one's foot, and one sank down through the body of some poor fellow.[89]

The practice of self censorship for the church audience at home may partly account for the seeming lack of moral or emotional struggle amongst these Free Church chaplains and the imbalance when presenting their gospel ministry successes. *Chaplains in Khaki* is a good example of this kind of literature. However, in spite of the criticisms, this book gives a vibrant account of the revivalism that took place amongst soldiers during the First World War and gives a clear idea of its effect.

Shakespeare, in his foreword to *Some Chaplains in Khaki* states that the reason for its publication was that "[t]he work of the United Board can only be completely effective as its existence and rights become a matter of common knowledge among His Majesty's Forces and if it receives the persistent and serious co-operation of our ministers and churches."[90] This book may well have been Shakespeare's idea for Spurr states in the introduction that he "had been asked to try and create a literary link between them [the chaplains] and the churches they represent at home, and the general Christian public."[91] One review firmly commended this book as an accurate description of "the evolution of the United Board, and in a series of vivid chapters exhibits the chaplains about their Master's business…[and it] is impossible to read Mr. Spurr's book without realising, that our chaplains are men whom God has specially called and equipped for the wonderful and fruitful service in which they are engaged."[92] However, John Moyles[93] asked how the idea for this book had come about and "referred at some length to the exception which had been taken to the volume by members of the Primitive Methodist Denomination."[94] In response to Moyles' concerns, Shakespeare stated "that it was never intended that the book should in any way be

[89] Alfred O'Rahilly, *The Padre of Trench Street*, (West Sussex: Diggory Press 2005), pp.57-58
[90] Spurr, *Chaplains in Khaki*, p.7
[91] Ibid, p.9
[92] Nicholas Notewell, "Impressions of Nicholas Notewell, 'Some Chaplains in Khaki,.'" *BT*, December 17th 1915, p.820
[93] Primitive Methodist minister and a denominational representative to the U.B.
[94] 'UB Minutes', 16th March 1916, p.45

an account of the work of the United Navy and Army Board, but that it was a book written by Mr Spurr for the Baptist Publication Department, and intended to represent the work [of the U.B.] from the Baptist point of view."[95] This may have been true, but the foreword to this book clearly infers that it is written for the "general Christian public."[96]

In 1918 a forty-eight page booklet was printed by the U.B. entitled *The United Navy, Army and Air force Board: the Story of its Origin and Work* written by John Oxenham which may have been an attempt to reflect the work of the denominations it represented more accurately to meet Moyles' concerns and to indicate "a little of the efforts and the sacrifices of the chaplains during 1914-1918."[97] The Primitive Methodists may have been satisfied with these responses but the United Methodists obviously were not as they commissioned their own history in 1917 entitled *Stories from the Front by United Methodist Chaplains.* Henry Smith was the Editor and his hope was that "what is written will deepen the interest of the reader in the social, moral and spiritual well-being of our soldiers...[and]...deepen their admiration for a fine body of men such as Great Britain never had in its Army before."[98] This book was a collection of testimonies written by United Methodist chaplains describing their distressing ministry at the front. These testimonies manage to convey the awe fullness of war and the challenges of their ministry within it.

Apart from the officially sponsored histories there was the occasional autobiographical account. The most famous United Board memoirs were written by Phil Fisher a serving Primitive Methodist. His *Khaki Vignettes* became a very popular book probably because of the honest way it was written and the real sense of immediacy it conveyed. Fisher in his forward states that the book was the ...product of all sorts of odd moments and unhelpful situations. Some of it has been written in trenches, some in a tent or a rough bivouac, some in the train, some in the mess-room, to the accompaniment of a gramophone and much animated conversation. More than one chapter came to a chill birth in a hut whose temperature rendered my fingers nearly insensible to the pen; I doubt if any man wrote to his best inspiration when he was cold![99]

This work was later supplemented with his *Figures and Phases of the War 1916-1919* published around 1920 which simply shared his experience of the war

---

[95] Ibid, p.45
[96] Spurr, *Chaplains in Khaki*, p.7
[97] Thomson, *Ministering to the Forces*, p.17
[98] Ed: Henry Smith, *Stories from the Front*, p.12
[99] Fisher, *Khaki Vignettes*, Forward

through his own art work.[100]

Apart from these creative initiatives the leadership of the U.B. was deeply concerned about the continuing practice of Free Churchmen being attested to the wrong denomination by the Recruiting Sergeant on joining the service. This was to be a significant difficulty which the U.B. needed to address as the War Office was willing to commission Free Church chaplains only if the numbers signing up warranted it. Obviously, if those signing up were attested wrongly then it meant that fewer Free Church chaplains could be commissioned and it also allowed critics opportunity to accuse the Free Churches of not supporting the war effort effectively. This, in turn, would affect their prestige. The problem was "that young men enlist, the recruiting sergeant tells them it is no use putting themselves down on the attestation form as belonging to either the one denomination or the other, as there are no chaplains."[101] Spurr describes some of these difficulties:

> Scores of cases came to our knowledge in which the wishes of Free Churchmen to be registered according to their own denomination were ignored. They were put down as 'Church of England' against their protest, or some-times told that 'fancy religions' were not recognised. In some cases men who asked that they might attend their own church on Sunday were either sent to the Church of England Service *or put upon fatigue duty.*[102]

This kind of activity was well described within the U.B. Minutes for 10th November 1915. It was alleged that during one such parade service the "Free Churchmen fall out at one of the billets, for the Nonconformist service. From them they select the men to fetch rations: there are only two or three men left, so there is no parade."[103]

This practice of wrongfully attesting servicemen to the Church of England or occasionally to the Wesleyans had larger implications. George Standing C.F.(U.B.) commented "that the Board was at a great disadvantage through defective registration, and that in some Divisions the Wesleyans[104] were acting 'in

---

[100] Fisher, Phil J. *Figures and Phases of the War 1916-1919*, (London: Odhams Ltd,) c.1920
[101] 'Jottings,' *SBM*, 40.10, October 1914, p.154
[102] Spurr, *Chaplains in Khaki*, p.26
[103] 'UB Minutes,' 10th November 1915, p.325
[104] Peris Williams, a Congregationalist, also comments about the territorial attitude of some 'Wesleyan' chaplains. One, Williams records, "alleged that I had no right to call upon any Wesleyan - regardless of whether they were Welshmen." Peris Williams, *Diary of the Rev Peris Williams, Army Chaplain, 1914 - 16*, (The Website for Welsh Cultural History Visited 06/04/2005), p.60

an awkward manner'"[105] when he attempted to correctly re-register U.B. soldiers. T. N. Tattersall C.F.(U.B.) believed he could easily detect a 'Nonconformist' simply by the way he spoke. He writes: "Of heaven and hell, of sin and death and judgement one rarely hears him [the British soldier] speak. If he does speak of these things, or of conversion, or of the spiritual life, I know him at once. He is a Nonconformist. Perhaps his identification disc says, C. of E., but his speech betrayed him."[106] However, it could be far from humorous. Sadly, wrong denominational registration could occasionally have tragic consequences. Peris Williams C.F.(U.B.) writes bitterly in his diary about such an incident. He records that while visiting the injured at the military hospital at Loos he came across a young lad by the name of Lloyd and visited him regularly. Williams writes that "Lloyd the boy who was shot in the neck died. He was a Baptist (from Penrhiwceibr) who had been registered C of E. The C of E buried him although they had never visited him."[107] Williams had been visiting him regularly for a month and had got to know this fellow Welsh speaker and Nonconformist. This may explain his frustration.[108] Spurr was therefore right and naturally concerned to "urge our Ministers to make it known that those joining up can register in their own denominations; for we "are aware that great numbers from our congregations have been entered against their express wish under other denominations."[109]

The importance of this issue of attestation can be seen from the research done by one particular chaplain who found that in a division of seven thousand men there were surprisingly "very few if any Free Churchman... It has been on vitiated statistics that any charges of slackness in army service that have been brought against Nonconformists have been unfounded - and they are now shown to be false."[110] This difficulty of being wrongly attested would later cause difficulties for the Baptist Union of Scotland who wanted, through the U.B, to gain chaplains for Scottish Divisions. They needed five hundred U.B. attestations if they were to get any chaplains[111] but despite the large numbers of Scottish Baptists who were enlisting into Scottish Battalions, there were no Nonconformist chaplains to serve their needs. Thomas Jones, an army chaplain, was seeking to gain two U.B. chaplains to be able to serve with the Scottish Divisions and the Scottish Baptist Church Council was looking into this matter. However this was not a major concern for the U.B. and the Scottish Regiments remained in the hands of the

---

105 'UB Minutes,' September 22nd 1915, p.287
106 T. N. Tattersall, 'The British Soldier in Hospital,' *BT*, April 9th 1915, p.235
107 Peris Williams, *Diary*, p.65
108 Ibid, p.64
109 Ibid, p.8
110 'Jottings,' *SBM*, December 1915, p.187
111 'Jottings,' *SBM*, October 1916, p.162

Scottish Presbyterians for the duration of the Great War even though they were struggling to recruit.[112] There was, though, a great deal of interest in "securing (the U.B's) proper rights and status"[113] within the British Army of India. It was recorded as early as 1915 that A. E. Hubbard of Bombay was concerned that "(m)any of our Nonconformists are down as Church of England and no matter how we try we cannot obtain correct returns. I think something ought to be done to secure trustworthy returns from our four denominations. I think the time has come to place our military work out here in India on a sound basis."[114] He believed that the "scruples of men… had been ignored."[115] Shakespeare requested an interview, as U.B. representative, with the Indian Office to discuss this deeply concerning issue.

The Indian Army was not the U.B.'s only concern. Harry Martin Brown C.F.(U.B.) was a member of staff at Calabar College Kingston in Jamaica, West Indies, before being commissioned as an army chaplain. He was passionate about the spiritual care and welfare of the West Indian soldiers he had responsibility for, the majority of whom were U.B. He had insisted that he be allowed to serve with West Indian troops and in 1917 was attached to 4th Battalion The British West Indies Regiment and was posted immediately to the Front in France. Writing to Shakespeare while being shipped to France, Brown tells of the enormous opportunities that were his on the SS Bermudian and raises the controversial question of denominational proportions. He wrote:

> You will realise the greatness of the opportunity when I tell you that out of 800 men on ""SS Bermudian"" from Jamaica recently, 500 were Baptist, Congregational and Methodist. As I am the only U.B. padre attached to the W.I. (West Indian) troops I would like to get into touch with all our men out in France. Some are in Egypt where they are also without a padre. The recent appointment of six C-of-E and one U.B. Chaplain was certainly a wrong proportion. The majority of our men are nonconformist, and they are people who strongly object to any changes. They particularly need their own kind of Chaplain, and one discovers more every day how imperative it is that the padre thoroughly understands the native. We have riot upon riot lately merely because the officers in charge do not know how to handle the natives.[116]

---

112 Michael Snape, *The Royal Army Chaplain's Department: Clergy Under Fire*, pp.197-198
113 'UB Minutes,' 9th May 1917, p.271
114 'UB Minutes,' 10th June 1915, p.240
115 Ibid, p.240
116 WO374/9800 Henry Martin Brown cited by Shakespeare in a letter to Geoffrey Monk Esq 5th September 1917

Though this issue was brought up with the War Office by Shakespeare no change in proportions occurred and West Indian battalions continued to be served primarily by Church of England chaplains. Brown's description of constant riots reveals that West Indian soldiers were deeply unhappy with the way they were being treated and one of these concerns was religious affiliation. Brown wrote to Shakespeare again on 11th July 1918 from Craiglochart Hospital for Officers in Edinburgh, while recovering from shell shock that he had received during the Arras Offensive,[117] and asked if he might be posted to Kingston and Port Royal in Jamaica to work amongst West Indian troops garrisoned there rather, than waste his time being sick in England. The reason for wishing to serve in Jamaica was that "There is great scope for a Baptist chaplain because so many of our men are Baptist, [for] at the present moment we are without a Minister at East Queens Street, Kingston."[118] It could be argued that Brown's concern should have been taken more seriously by Shakespeare and the U.B. than was evident, even if the A.Ch.D. was not supportive. However the question of chaplaincy cover for 'coloured troops' had been raised by Shakespeare and presented to the Army Council in January 1917[119]. It is not recorded what the answer was but it is obvious that one U.B. chaplain was considered enough cover for the 'coloured troops,' an inequality which Brown would later complain about. Obviously, Shakespeare saw the U.B.'s remit as Empire wide and not just concerned with the interests of the British military.

The appointment of chaplains from the Church of England being attached to largely 'Free Church' regiments was also a concern for those serving within the British forces. A 'soldier' wrote to the U.B. complaining that "Months ago our Nonconformist Padre was taken from us, and we have only had the C of E man, although, the Unit is eighty per cent Nonconformist. I'm sorry to say he seems better suited for any profession but the one he holds, and probably because of that, the inspiration we got in the dark days of Suvla[120] has disappeared and there is

[117] The battle of Arras 1917 was a major British attack on long established German positions in Artois, east of Arras. The attack opened on 9 April, after a five-day, 2,800-gun PRELIMANARY BOMBARDMENT that sacrificed any hope of surprise. Fourteen British divisions advanced along a line held by six divisions of the German Sixth Army" The offensive finished on the 3rd May 1917. "The battle as a whole was seen by Allied commanders as a relative success. Vimy Ridge was considered an important gain, and BEF losses of about 150,000 men, against an estimated 100,000 German casualties, represented a better ratio of attrition than usual for attackers on the Western Front." Pope & Wheal, *Dictionary*, p.37

[118] Letter: Brown to Shakespeare 11th July 1918

[119] 'UB Minutes,' 11th January 1917, p.207

[120] The Suvla Bay Offensive was the main Allied summer offensive on the GALLIPOLI FRONT in 1915. The offensive opened on 6 August and immediately lost cohesion. A full scale attack was attempted which broke down completely by 10 August. The offensives cost about 18,000 Allied

scarcely any interest taken by any of us in these matters."[121] Thomas Jones C.F.(U.B.) who was then based in Egypt, was requested to look into the situation and report back to the U.B. The intense debate concerning the correct recording of denominational proportions continued. There was so much concern about it, within Baptist circles, that in 1917 the Baptist Union of Great Britain Council argued for a Baptist Navy and Army Church. The laudable aim for such a body was to help support "those serving in His Majesty's forces at home or abroad who were already members of a Baptist Church and others who desire to become members on the following basis: a declaration before God, of faith in our Lord Jesus Christ, and of a desire to follow him and to do His will."[122] This was because Baptists were constantly annoyed about the continued inaccurate recording of denominational allegiance. However the other denominational colleagues represented in the U.B. felt it undermined the joint Union and so this initiative was not taken further. Another initiative by the U.B. to make sure soldiers were correctly attested was to give them the right to change their attestation when in hospital "and it was resolved that, in the event of a case being brought before the notice of the United Board where a soldier was not permitted to re-register, it should be taken up with the war office authorities."[123]

Shakespeare took his duty of care towards the U.B. chaplains seriously and decided to visit them at the 'Front' in France for ten days, although he did not enter the trenches. During this visit he was the guest of the Principal Chaplain and Major General Simms who showed him every kindness, and even put his car at Shakespeare's disposal and personally showed him around.[124] A. T. Guttery C.F.(U.B.) serving at the 'Front' at the time of Shakespeare's visit, saw these visits as evidence that the U.B. had come in out of the cold and had gained the recognition that normally was reserved only for Anglican dignitaries. He writes that "Bishops had been out to visit the Anglicans, and distinguished people of all sorts to visit the other denominations, but we had not been so highly favoured. *Now* we can hold up our heads with pride as we think of the effect he created."[125] This duty of care by the U.B. was also reflected in a letter that was sent to all the denominations being served by the U.B. which pointed out the opportunity afforded to the churches to minister to the welfare of the home coming soldiers, especially those wholly or partially disabled... it further urged upon churches the advisability of instituting look-out committees to watch for opportunities to thus

---

casualties. See Pope & Wheal, *Dictionary*, pp.458-459

[121] 'UB Minutes,' 14th September 1916, p.148

[122] 'Baptist Union Council minutes,' 20 Nov 1917

[123] 'UB Minutes,' 17th December 1915, p.331

[124] 'UB Minutes,' 11th January 1917, p.206

[125] J. Wallett. 'The Rev. A. T. Guttery at the Front.' *BT*, October 15th 1915, p.664

befriend the men and enable them to feel that the Church indeed seeks to be their helper."[126]

In 1917 the U.B. came to the fore of internationalism when it was made responsible for arranging the spiritual care of United States troops based in Europe. The high number of congregationally governed churches within the U.S. forces was the reason for the U.B. being given this additional prestige, although no details remain of the work achieved. In the same year Lord Derby had received 'representations' concerning pastoral care for the 'British Interned' held in Switzerland which alleged that it "was not entirely suitable or adequate."[127] In April 1917 an experienced chaplain Frank Fairfax C.F.(U.B.)[128] had been appointed to serve the British interned in Switzerland[129] partly recommended because he "had a tendency to consumption."[130] His work was appreciated and on the 24th September 1918 he was appointed Honorary Chaplain to the Forces after he relinquished his commission.[131] Whereas previously the U.B. had been considered a minor, though important player in national affairs, it had now been elevated to a more significant position on the international scene.

Shakespeare, as Chairman of the U.B., complained in January 1918 that "a disproportionate number of decorations were awarded to Anglican chaplains."[132] Shakespeare's protests were accepted and a supplementary New Year's Honours List was hurriedly published. Wilkinson comments: "who would have predicted before the war that dissenters would be petitioning for more honours from the military establishment?"[133] Shakespeare had brought the Free Church in from the cold. This great leader and organiser would settle for nothing less than total equality in all areas with the Church of England, and total equality meant equal recognition in the honours list too. Most U.B. chaplains were also awarded an 'Honorary Chaplain to the Forces' title (H.C.F) on relinquishing their commission. The U.B. actually suggested that H.C.F.s should be "gazetted in order that their status might be made secure."[134] Official recognition was immensely important because it revealed their significance in post war society after being persecuted and discriminated against in the past. Long after the Great War had finished the

[126] 'UB Minutes,' 29th November 1917
[127] 'UB Minutes,' 11th January 1917, p.208
[128] Pte Frank Fairfax, of the 18th Battalion West Yorkshire Regiment, was promoted from the ranks on the 23rd June 1915.
[129] 'UB Minutes,' 20th April 1917, p.251
[130] Letter Monk to Shakespeare 9th May 1918 WO339/138021
[131] Letter A. C. Strange to F. Fairfax 24th September 1918 W0339/138021
[132] Robinson, 'Role,' p.47
[133] Wilkinson, *Dissent of Conform?* p.39
[134] 'UB Minutes,' 25th September 1918, p.264

U.B. was still following up the matter of awards. Ernest Payne who would become Secretary of the U.B., as late as 1957, was trying to follow up J. C. Rendall's awards for his service during World War One so that he could wear them to "take part in the Remembrance Service at the War Memorial."[135] Honours and medals were tangible evidence of the important service that Free Church chaplains provided during the war and with their recognition the prestige and influence of the Free Churches was enhanced.

The United Board's attention was soon directed to the demobilization of its chaplains. It was deemed important to get these pastors released as soon as possible to take up the leadership of their churches once again. Under the direction of J. Penry Davey, the Principle United Board chaplain, the following scheme was adopted:

1. A list of Demobilization Camps to be sent to each of the representatives on the Interdenominational Advisory Committee.

2. A room shall be provided in each Discharge Centre at which every soldier shall meet a Chaplain or other representative of his Church.

3. The Chaplain to prepare a nominal roll of all United Board men, and to send their names to the A.P.C. of the Command.

4. The A.P.C. to send the names to the Principal Chaplain, who himself will send them to the respective Denominations constituting the United Board.[136]

Throughout the war the U.B. remained the major influence on chaplains and strongly influenced even their postings and promotions. The U.B. also took responsibility for providing to its chaplains headed paper on which to write their official letters.[137] Shepherd believes that the U.B. "was only one factor among many in the long process of the integration of Nonconformity into national life, but it made a significant contribution to the process, and is illustrative of how it occurred."[138] Soon there would be another committee where the Free Church voice could be heard. The 'Interdenominational Advisory Committee' was set up to make sure that all the denominations represented within the chaplaincy team could openly talk through issues and find just solutions for those concerns.

---

[135] WO374/56924 J. C. Rendall C.F.; Letter E. A. Payne to the D.C.G. Lloyd Evans 2nd October 1957.
[136] 'UB Minutes,' 4th December 1918, p.357
[137] 'UB Minutes,' 8th July 1915, p.242
[138] Shepherd, *The Making of a Modern Denomination*, p.101

IV. The Interdenominational Advisory Committee

The A.Ch.D. was growing, especially when serving chaplains were bolstered by the recruitment of 'Temporary' chaplains, and each denomination was demanding the recruitment of their own denominational chaplains to look after their own soldiers. The Church of England responded to the constant pressure by the Free Churches by forming the 'Advisory Committee on Church of England Chaplains' to look after the interests of the Anglican Church as well as being a useful committee for dealing with their own internal disputes. Naturally the formation of this committee was not welcomed by the Free Churches and was considered by them to be a threat to their newly acquired prestige. It was the Church of Scotland who first raised its concerns through the influential Lord Balfour, a War Office representative and Chairman of the Presbyterian Chaplaincy Committee. Balfour strongly believed that the Presbyterians were being disadvantaged by the Church of England's actions and he resigned from his post making the strength of feeling very clear. This, along with the complaints by the U.B. about unequal treatment, led Lloyd George to look for an acceptable solution.[139] That solution would be to create an Interdenominational Advisory Committee (I.A.C.) which would help deal effectively with the 'sensitivities' of the various denominations making up the A.Ch.D. On 18th July 1916 Lloyd George asked for proposed representatives to form this I.A.C. Amusingly the Free Churches which made up the U.B. initially struggled to agree upon who would represent the U.B. thus revealing a certain lack of unity. This is not too surprising as the U.B. recognised a number of very different churches and at the end of the war it had represented twelve Free Church denominations.[140] Lord Derby was appointed to chair this new committee which held its first meeting at the war office on the 18th August 1916.[141] Shakespeare was concerned that the committee would be ineffective unless denominational equality was first established. On behalf of the U.B. he wrote to the War Office arguing that:

The inequalities of treatment have become so serious in the case of non-Anglican churches that there would be no hope of the Interdenominational Committee working harmoniously for the welfare of the troops unless these were put right to begin with. We have not to discuss these matters with the Church of England, or to beg our rights from it, but with the War Office and with this as a preliminary statement, we should start on the level.[142]

---

[139] Ibid, p.97
[140] Robinson, 'Role,' p.27
[141] 'IAC minutes,' 18th August 1916
[142] Robinson, 'Role,' p.32; See also Thompson, 'Free Church,' p.337

In spite of Shakespeare's reservations, the first meeting of the I.A.C. debated a number of issues which addressed many of the inequalities felt by the Free Churches. The I.A.C., for example swiftly took up the issue of the "Non C/E" suffix being given to non-Anglican Senior Chaplains in France.[143] M'Clymont could not understand why Free Churchmen should be defined by the norm of the Church of England. He was concerned that it would give the impression that the Free Churches were not as "credible" as the Church of England. He argued that it would be far better if the Church of England was noted with the suffix "C/E" and the "Non C/E" suffix dropped. The Chaplain General was not in favour[144] because of his determination not to lose any prestige for the Church of England, and it was his view that was carried. Therefore, other discussions, for example, on chaplain's dress codes, like the I.A.C. recommendation that "shoulder straps of non-C-of-E Chaplains should be purple instead of black,"[145] had an importance beyond the mere cosmetic.

There is an interesting discussion concerning correct attestation amongst Mackay, the Chaplain General and Shakespeare which reflects a real sense of tension, resentment and the different ways their responsibilities were understood. At this first I.A.C. meeting Dr Mackay said he thought that an English Division was not predominantly Church of England than a Scottish Division was predominantly Presbyterian. The Chaplain General disagreed, and quoted as a similar case the Welsh (38th Division) which was alleged to be Non-Conformist, but was shown by official statistics to be largely Anglican. The Chairman pointed out that owing to the form of attestation, such official figures, were, according to his own experience, entirely worthless.[146]

In answer to a question by Mr Shakespeare the chairman said the Welsh Division would be regarded as 'typically non-Anglican'

The Minutes of the meeting record that the "The Chaplain General demurred to this scheme as not giving a sufficient establishment to the Church of England. He said official statistics could not be ignored and the Church of England held itself responsible for spiritual ministration to all who had entered the Army as belonging to that Church."[147] This badly recorded discussion helps us to see the very real tensions between the different denominational representatives on the I.A.C. and the resentment of the Church of England towards the encroaching influence of the

---

143 'IAC Minutes,' 13th October 1916
144 Thompson, 'Free Churches,' pp.348-349
145 IAC decision recorded in 'UB Minutes' 20th April 1917
146 'IAC Minutes,' 18th August 1916
147 Ibid

Free Churches on its historic territory.

The attendance list for the 10th November notes the attendance of the following, including Shakespeare.

Lord Derby (in the Chair)
Sir R H Brade (Vice Chairman)
The Chaplain General (C of E)
Dr J A M'Clymont (C of S)
Dr P B Mackay (United Free Church of Scotland)
Revd J Grierson (Presbyterian Church of England)
Mgr M Bidwell (RC)
Revd J H Bateson (Wesleyan Methodists)
Revd J H Shakespeare (Baptist UB)
Revd H Elvet Lewis (Welsh Calvinistic Methodists)

Dr W MacKean represented Irish Presbyterians although he had not attended the above meeting[148]

The A.I.C. continued to seek to correct inequalities between the Church of England, the Roman Catholic Church and the Free Churches. There was general concern about the disproportionate growth of Church of England chaplains in France. At the beginning of the war there were, for example: thirty-one with the relative rank of Colonel (C.F.1.), twenty-five of these being Church of England; five with the relative rank of Lt. Colonel (C.F.2.), two being Church of England and three Roman Catholic; thirty-five with the relative rank of Major (C.F.3.) twenty-five being Church of England. Out of the thirty-three of those with the relative rank of Captain (C.F.4.), twenty-nine were Church of England. This obviously led to the promotion of Church of England chaplains and the non-promotions of Free Church chaplains. Lord Derby, in response, proposed a new structure for non Anglican Chaplains. He proposed:

One A.C.G. (Assistant Chaplain General) for each Army and Main Base
One D.P.C. (Depute Principal Chaplain) for each Army Corps
One Senior Chaplain for each Division

These posts might be held by any non-Anglican Denomination. Selection was based upon years of service and administrative ability. This had the practical effect of splitting the A.Ch.D. into leadership patterns that represented their own differing denominations. During this period it was important for the Free Churches to change their administrative patterns to be able to respond to any risk of losing

[148] Thompson, 'Free Church,' p.342

their prestige or becoming dominated, once again, by the Church of England. If any disputes occurred then the I.A.C. was in place to mediate.

Lord Derby also ensured a more balanced spread of Chaplains across the Divisions. The table below shows the new distribution of chaplains in each Division. Thus, for example, each English Division had nine Anglican chaplains, four Roman Catholic and four Independent/ Presbyterians/ U.B./ Methodists.[149]

	Eng. Divisions	Scot. Divisions	South Irish Divisions
C/E	9	4	5
R/C	4	4	9
Presb.	-	9	-
Presb. Or Noncon	4	-	4

(Quoted by J.H. Thompson, 'Free Church,' pp.346-7)

These changes, which would be accepted by the War Office, led to the U.B. gaining 174 chaplains by the beginning of 1917. This was made up of 61 Baptists and 59 Congregationalists, 27 Primitive Methodists and 27 United Methodists. Most applications for recognition by unrecognised denominations applied to the U.B. to gain recognition within the military. This meant the U.B. along with the I.A.C. had the difficult task of deciding the suitability of the applicant presented by a denomination not yet recognised by the U.B. One of their first challenges was to decide if Salvation Army Officers could be commissioned as military chaplains. Shakespeare opposed their inclusion on the grounds that:

i. it was desirable to confine chaplaincy appointments to recognised churches;
ii. it would be difficult to guarantee the qualification of Salvation Army nominees;
iii. the Salvation Army was concerned more with social than religious questions, and
iv. Bodies such as the Church Army were in a similar position.[150]

Like the Church Army, the Salvation Army was a para-church organisation rather than a church and because it could not offer the sacraments, an outward sign

[149] Ibid, pp.346-7
[150] Ibid, p.356

which Christ gave to his church it could not be considered a church denomination. However, in spite of the I.A.C.'s and Shakespeare's opposition five Salvation Army Officers were appointed as chaplains to the Western Front in France. The Unitarians, however, were refused as "unacceptable" by the I.A.C.[151] Thompson believes that there was a disinclination by the Free Churchman on the I.A.C. "to support the chaplaincy bids of churches not represented there"[152] already. Whether this disinclination did exist or not, the I.A.C. and especially the U.B. element, were happy to look positively at an application of a young Moravian Minister serving within the ranks of the Royal Scots (The Royal Regiment) and commended by Bishop Hasse. The Bishop, in the letter commending this minister, asked "whether, in view of the fact that 20% of the members of the Moravian Church had enlisted... Could an OCF be appointed under the UB?" It was felt by the U.B. that the request was a very reasonable one"[153] Shakespeare and Wells, therefore, interviewed this Moravian Minister, a L.Cpl. Paul F. Horton of the 15th Bn. R.S., and agreed to approach the War Office to release him to Chaplaincy work. Sadly, he did not survive long enough to become a chaplain for he died of wounds before being transferred.[154] The news of his death was "received with deep regret by the Board."[155] However, at the meeting of the U.B. on 25th September 1918 G. W. Macleavery, another Moravian Minister was proposed and accepted[156] to serve as a chaplain under the direction of the U.B. It was not altogether correct when Thompson stated that "In relation to the churches not represented, the Committee themselves were in danger of appearing as a new privileged group..."[157] For although the U.B. did reject similar requests by other denominations it was always because their numbers were too small to justify their recruitment (as with the Wesleyan Reform Union)[158] or they considered the applicant to be unorthodox, (as with the Unitarians) or a non church, (as with the Salvation Army). The Board's readiness to accept a Moravian minister reveals clearly its willingness to be open to working closely with other denominations.

Apart from religious issues the I.A.C. debated a number of social concerns related to military conduct and other church related issues such as:

1."Foul and blasphemous language" often used by SNCO's on the parade

[151] Ibid, p.357 citing the Methodist Forces Board papers 1/2 and 3/17
[152] Ibid, p.356
[153] 'UB Minutes,' 29th June 1916
[154] Thompson, 'Free Church, ' p.357 See also the War Graves Commission details: Horton, Paul Fredrick Died of Wounds on 28th September 1917 and is buried in West-Vlaaderen Belgium
[155] 'UB Minutes, ' 29th November 1917
[156] 'UB Minutes,' 25th September 1918
[157] Thompson, 'Free Church, ' p.369
[158] 'UB Minutes,' 29th November 1917

squares[159]
2. The playing of Sunday Sports which often affected the serviceman's desire for Sunday observance as did military training. The Royal Flying Corps also often used Sundays for flight training.[160]
3. Brothels and London Prostitutes.[161]
4. Purity or the fight against venereal disease.

Shakespeare initially raised the purity issue and this became a main concern of the Board. They sought to provide professional and knowledgeable speakers who would speak directly to the troops concerning the dangers and temptations facing them. This would be a great support to the chaplains' work in local bases. The committees' lectures were put in a handbook and published under the title of the "Cornerstone of Reconstruction."[162]

Another issue which was, not surprisingly, addressed by the I.A.C. was the issue of alcohol and its ill effects on those serving at the 'Front.' After all had not David Lloyd George himself declared in 1915 that "We are fighting Germany, Austria and Drink, and the greatest of these deadly foes is Drink."[163] Certainly this was a major concern for many Free Churchmen brought up with strong ethics that commended sobriety, so obviously they would be deeply concerned about the amount of alcohol being allowed to the Front. This was a war within a war. Certainly British Nonconformist pressure nearly succeeded in a "total prohibition movement in order... to help the war effort."[164] These protests were eventually ignored.

Another, very important social change during this time that would eventually have a significant effect upon the military was the changing role of women which led to the creation of the Women's Army Auxilliary Corps (W.A.A.C.). The W.A.A.C. was a support arm for those serving at the Front and the implications for such an organization were discussed by the I.A.C.[165] though not in detail nor often. They obviously did not see its importance, though they did support this new initiative. The main concerns of the A.I.C. were: how could the work of the W.A.A.C. be promoted? How might they "bring the Chaplaincy Service into relationship with

[159] Ibid, p.361
[160] Ibid, p.361
[161] Ibid, p.362
[162] Ibid, pp.364-366
[163] Ruston, 'Attitudes, ' p.254
[164] Ruston, 'Baptist Nonconformist,' p.254
[165] 'IAC Minutes,' 1st February 1918

the W.A.A.C."?[166] and the old sensitive issue of the correct attestation of those women joining up.

The U.B. sought to keep its own standards high concerning the selection of chaplains. After all they wanted to gain official recognition and the prestige and opportunities that this recognition afforded. This would not have been possible if its chaplains were unfit and lacking in some moral or pastoral quality. It would be accurate to refer to the U.B. at this time as unashamedly elitist. To keep these high standards the U.B. formed a Chaplaincy Selection Committee in 1917.[167] The first commissioned Baptist and Congregational chaplains had been deployed to France with the British Expeditionary Force on the 9th October 1914. Ernest Lodge Watson represented the Baptists and J.J.L. Clayton the Congregationalists. After the formation of the U.B. on the 14th January 1915 more chaplains would swiftly follow. On joining, the Army Chaplain was entitled to a pay advance equivalent to thirty days pay (a Chaplain's wage was ten Shillings a day), a field communion set, service books, a batman and a horse and saddlery. The Chaplain could expect a gratuity of sixty days pay when contract obligations were completed.[168]

V. The National Climate

Britain's declaration of war on Germany and her allies on the 4th August 1914 was greeted by intense patriotic fervour and there was not much difference in approach whether Free Church, Established Church or Roman Catholic. In *Christian World,* a Free Church journal, the editor concludes: "In the present conflict it is clear that we are not fighting against the scientific acumen, the philosophical or theological learning of Germany, nor, indeed, against the German people as such, but against the manifestation of the Anti-Christ which expresses itself in the masterful, the imperious and the power-loving Zeitgeist."[169] J. T. Forbes in his article entitled 'The Recruiting Call' published in the *Scottish Baptist Magazine* of December 1915 argued that Free Churchman should join up on the grounds that:

> If any was ever justified this war is.... Force can be sanctified just as suffering can be sanctified. It sanctified to win civil and religious freedom, to destroy the slave trade, to rescue missionaries from Burmese, and later from Abyssinian captivity; to purge the United States from slavery. It is being sanctified to-day to oppose the treaty breakers and war makers of

[166] 'IAC Minutes,' 1st February 1918
[167] Snape, *Royal Army Chaplain's Department,* p.200
[168] See War Office Clergy Gen. No.4044 form
[169] Ibid, pp.243 -244

Germany.....It is a question of contending in arms unto blood, striving against sin; the sin that would wreck the gains of civilisation, and substitute, wherever prevailing, for Christian standard the rule of might, justifying itself by the mere fact of victory.....And the man who answers at once will know that he has had his part in the victorious contest that is to give us, we pray God, a purified and ennobled nation and a new and Christianised European life.[170]

Forbes believed in "such a thing as sanctified force." He continued confidently that "Christian ethics can be a spur as well as a curb."[171] This kind of rhetoric raised the war above simple national interests to an idealised fight on the side of good against evil. The war "is the clash of two totally different and quite irreconcilable ideals. On the one side is the ideal to which mankind has been painfully climbing, that love and righteousness are the law in the life of nations as truly as in the life of individuals. On the other is the ideal, openly announced by German philosophers, statesmen and soldiers, that brute strength, reinforced by science, is supreme in international relationships."[172]

Those going to serve within the forces also felt the just cause of the war and T. N. Tattersall[173] was very clear that the British nation was "up against a foe capable of waging the most deadly warfare, and most unscrupulous in its methods - a foe capable of bombarding defenceless towns; a foe capable of torturing prisoners of war, and murdering our wounded on the field of battle; a devilish and fiendish foe, who slew defenceless women and children. The world would not breathe easily again until the wild beast had been caged and his teeth and claws drawn."[174] If any war was justified then, according to Tattersall, this one was. He outlined his views even more robustly in an article entitled 'The Day of Battle.' He argued that if one wants evidence that a devil exists then study the philosophy of the enemy: "Arm-chair philosophers, or saints that sit at ease in Zion, may scout the existence of the devil, but at the front we are less sceptical. If we do not see him, we behold his works."[175] His evidence for these views was the sheer horror of war, when "hundreds of bright-eyed, clean-limbed, stout-hearted young men are mown down like grass by machine guns, blown into the air by shells, pierced through and through with steel, and all because of an Emperor's insensate ambition to become

---

[170] J. T. Forbes, 'The Recruiting Call,' *SBM*, 41.12, December 1915, pp.186-187
[171] J. T. Forbes, 'Sildartite,' *The Baptist Handbook 1916*, p.267
[172] *BT*, 11th September 1914
[173] For a fuller understanding of Tattersall's ministry read Neil E. Allison 'T. N. Tattersall D.S.O: His War Experience and Medals,' *The RAChD Journal* Vol. 45, 2006
[174] T. N. Tattersall, 'Chaplain Tattersall on Furlough,' *BT*, July 16th 1915, p.472
[175] T. N. Tattersall, 'The Day of Battle,' *SBM*, 41.5, May 28th 1915, p.347

Lord of Europe, we say 'An evil spirit hath done this.'"[176] No wonder an anonymous Free Church recruit declared in the pages of the *Baptist Times* that "I stood for independence and freedom. How many times from public platforms have I exhorted the working classes to regard every German as a brother? Now I am paying for it all. The bugle has sounded, and after a few months under canvas I emerge a disappointed Liberal, and with no feelings of brotherhood against the Kaiser. However, I am still a strong Baptist!"[177]

William Cramb Charteris C.F.(U.B.)[178] another prominent army chaplain looked upon the soldiers of his division and remarked that he "felt assured of two things:-

1 The righteousness of our cause.
2 The assurance of ultimate and complete victory."[179]

Naturally, these diatribes against the 'evil Hun' often led to the common parallel of the cowardly German and the brave Tommy. Charteris wrote, after visiting the wounded, that "Oh, the horror and crime of war, wounding and maiming our bravest and best sons and brothers. I have often heard of the stoical German, but they made more fuss than our men, though less severely wounded and showed great terror when the shells came nearer than usual. I felt proud to be a Britisher."[180] G. E. Minnear C.F.(U.B.) obviously held the same views. He wrote, while visiting the wounded during the Somme Offensive in 1916, that "(t)here also are many wounded Germans. Some of them bear their pain patiently, but the majority of them are cowards compared with our British boys. Their wounds are no worse, but they wince and grimace and writhe and groan under the most gentle treatment."[181] Although he does at least recognise one key difference. He wrote that "they may have been led to expect brutality and are consequently nervous."[182]

These temporary chaplains, who were obligated to serve for one year, joined an army whose volunteer ethos would be fairly tolerant of their religious practices even if some of their clerical colleagues looked on them with some degree of suspicion. The Chaplain General during this time of intense upheaval and radical change was the Evangelical Anglican clergymen and Bishop of Sierra Leone, John

[176] Ibid, p.347
[177] *BT*, 27th November 1914
[178] For a fuller understanding of Charteris's ministry read Neil E Allison 'Shakespeare's Man at the Front. The Rev. W. C. Charteris O.B.E. M.C.' *BQ* Vol. 41 No. 4 October 2005
[179] *SBM*, January 1918, p.4
[180] Charteris, 'Chaplains Work at the Front,' *SBM*, 44.1, January 1918, p.4
[181] *Stories from the Front*, p.25
[182] Ibid, p.25

Taylor Smith[183] (Chaplain General 1901 to 1925). He was favoured by Queen Victoria, which is not surprising since the "tone of Evangelicalism permeated nearly the whole of later Victorian religion outside the Roman Catholic Church..."[184] Taylor Smith was known for his active missionary work in a West African province of the Empire. He was able to keep the A.Ch.D. steady throughout this time of great turmoil[185] and develop its importance within government and military circles. Taylor Smith recognized that the war had brought men together from every kind of community and communion in the country. Their spiritual needs were as important to the Bishop as the provision of outfit, arms and ammunition. His job was to see that no man went into the trenches without having, close at hand, some word which would help him in his hours of danger and in the close approach of death... He (therefore) asked the bishops to lend to the War office the best men they had available for the duties of wartime chaplains.[186]

At times he would directly approach ministers if he thought they were suitable, as in the case of Charles Doudney.[187]

Taylor Smith helped create an atmosphere of denominational tolerance as long as chaplains had a living faith judged from his own Evangelical perspective, something that was important for Free Church men. Langston believes that "Taylor Smith was seeking for chaplains who fully realised that they were to be the spiritual advisors of men who would face death daily, and to whom each message delivered might be the last: or who, having dodged death, might become permanent moral wrecks unless warned and guarded."[188] In an interview with the *Daily Chronicle* Taylor Smith asserted that denomination is not important as far as 'Tommy' is concerned as long as he is able to receive the comfort of God from his own chaplain. In this article Taylor Smith said:

> All Protestant creeds are one in the fighting line. If an Anglican minister is not at hand, a Presbyterian speaks a few words, and all of the Protestant denominations work hand and glove... Only for Holy Communion in the field does he wear surplice, and usually he invites all, the unconfirmed, or

---

[183] Bishop Smith K.C.B. C.V.O. D.D. B:20th April 1860 - D:1938)

[184] D. W. Bebbington, *Evangelicalism in Modern Britain: A History from the 1730s to the 1980s*, (London: Unwin Hyman, 1989), p.2

[185] E. H. Thorold, 'The Right Reverend Bishop John Taylor Smith KCB CVO DD,' *RAChD Journal*, Vol. 6, No.46, July 1938, p.95

[186] Maurice Whitlow, *J. Taylor Smith K.C.B. C.V.O., D.D. Everybody's Bishop*, (London: Lutterworth Press, 1938), p.86

[187] Ed: Jonathan Horne, *The Best of the Goodfellows The Diaries and Memoirs of the Rev. Charles Edmund Doudney, M.A., C.F. (1871-1915)*, (Privately Published 1995), p.7

[188] E. L. Langston, *Bishop Taylor Smith*, (London: Marshall, Morgan & Scott, Ltd 1938), p.128

even those of other creeds, to participate, for any minute may mean death out there."[189]

However, his approach allowed the common accusation of favouring Anglican chaplains, and others of his own 'low church' disposition. His approach to chaplaincy recruitment shows the importance Smith placed upon evangelism and mission. The most important aspect of his vision for military chaplaincy was to save souls, and to achieve this he must obviously recruit 'the right sort,' that is chaplains who had a living faith.[190] Smyth reflects negatively on this and states: "Perhaps most of the Regular Chaplains were of this type (extreme low church) - many of them Protestant Irish men."[191] Padre Julian Bickersteth would have firmly agreed with Smyth. In July 1916 Bickersteth managed to attend the C.G.'s conference that was being held, at a safe distance, behind the lines. After listening attentively to the speeches of fellow chaplains, Bickersteth recorded that

> it soon became apparent…that the majority present were much after the Chaplain General's own heart. There were not more than a dozen moderate High Churchmen present. I had not realised before how successful the CG had been in appointing men of his own way of thinking. There were quite a few padres there with moustaches, and as they wore khaki collars they looked very much like combatant officers.[192]

The church generally, whether Established or Free, had a common hope and, often a common approach. The churches believed that this Great War would be the catalyst for a Christian revival, just like that fairly recently experienced (1904 and 1905) in Wales. "War was wrong, but it might, in evangelical thinking, be used to bring about what was right,"[193] and that positive outcome certainly included a revival.

The Welsh Revival of 1904-1905 was a significant influence on Free Church chaplains during this period. During this revival "many Christians became infused with missionary spirit and dedicated themselves to a holy life and not infrequently to cultural and social service"[194] especially under the charismatic leadership of Evan Roberts. This ex-coal miner "displayed all the characteristics of a

---

[189] William E. Sellers, *With Our Fighting Men*, (London: RTS 1916), pp.46-47
[190] See Langston, *Bishop Taylor Smith*, p.124
[191] John Smyth, *In this Sign Conquer*, (London: A. R. Mowbray & Co Ltd 1968), p.169
[192] Bickersteth, *The Bickersteth Diaries 1914-1918*, (London: Pen & Sword, 1995), p.81
[193] Randall, 'The Role of Conscientious Objectors,' p.10
[194] R. Tudor Jones, *Faith and the Crises of a Nation Wales 1890-1914*, (Cardiff: Univ. of Wales Press, 2004), p.283

charismatic prophet, enjoying direct contact with God, and thus receiving supernatural guidance...[for] the Salvation of Souls weighed heavily upon [him]. He felt on fire to go through the length and breadth of Wales to tell people about the Saviour."[195] As well as Evan Roberts, others such as William Booth, Gipsy Smith, F. B. Meyer and R. A. Torrey led missions which resulted in 'stirrings' being experienced where many professed a revitalized or a converting faith in Christ.[196] The Padres were considered, by many people, as the spearhead of this kind of mission. Indeed at the beginning of the war there was a common belief "that the emergency would 'win for Christ' those whom peace had insulated from the reach of the church."[197] This viewpoint obviously appealed to Free Church padres whose theology lent itself to mission and revivalism.

It is not surprising, therefore, that within Free Church circles, a real admiration of the willingness of the Nation to give freely to this national and spiritual call to defend a small nation against Germany's tyranny, for "they did not ask if it would pay, they did not stay to reason why, they signed their lives away for their country's defence and honour."[198] This included ministers[199] and ministerial students who "freely enlisted as both combatants and non combatants."[200] John Cattrall, a Congregationalist, was a ministerial student who joined the R.A.M.C. Ambulance service because he "wanted to maintain his ordination vows."[201] He was killed in action on the 24th March 1918. A combatant volunteer was Joseph Fleming who joined the Highland Light Infantry. He was 'heroically' killed in action on the 15th September 1916 while leading his men. In his obituary this ministerial student of the Scottish Baptist College was described as "an excellent preacher, an unmistakably devout and devoted follower of Christ. His death has been an unspeakable loss to all who were connected with him...he had...given great promise of making an excellent minister of the Gospel."[202] J. R. Fleming claimed that "a large number of ministers enlisted as soldiers, some dying heroically on the field. Students and probationers for the ministry did not as a rule

195 Tudor Jones, *Crises of a Nation*, p.292

196 Ibid, p.290

197 Thompson, *The Free Church Army Chaplain*, p.284

198 John MacBeath ,'Our Volunteer Army,' *SBM*, 42.6, June 1916, p.85

199 The Anglican Church did not allow ministers or ministerial students to join up as combatants. The Archbishop of Canterbury believed that "the role of an active combatant was incompatible with the position of anyone who sought and received Holy Orders." Cited by David Coulter, 'The Church of Scotland Chaplains of World War Two,' (Unpublished Ph.D. Thesis University of Edinburgh, 1993), p.3

200 Coulter, 'Church of Scotland,' p.3

201 *Congregational Yearbook*, 1916, p.65

202 'In Memoriam. 2nd Lieut. Joseph Fleming,' *SBM*, November 1916, pp.176-177

wait for the enactment of conscription, but freely offered themselves...,"[203] At the same time there was a long term opposition to conscription as an undue interference with an individual's conscience and liberty. Parliament "had no right to force men against their will to train to kill one another."[204] This sounds very principled but it does not reflect the fact that "(w)ithin families, clubs, churches, chapels or other social groups, young men found themselves required to explain why they were not volunteering."[205]

However by the end of 1915 it became clear that conscription was the only way the requirements for waging war would be met. In June 1916 conscription was made legal and every British male between the ages of 18 and 41 was liable to being called up. The giving up of the principle of volunteerism was presented in the *Baptist Times* as a necessary compromise, if not a positive one. The article argued that "We distrust Conscription, but we dread a German victory still more....."[206] Surprisingly this desire for national acceptance would find the U.B. supporting a letter sent to the 'various denominational authorities' from Sir Auckland Geddes representing the Ministry of National Service which stated:

> Before any man of military age is admitted to the ministry, particulars of the man in question should be sent to this Department, such particulars including information of the medical grade in which he has been placed and the place where he was examined, and that he should only be admitted to the ministry in the event of no objection being taken by this Department.[207]

It is interesting that no discussion is recorded concerning the 'call' to ministry being subjugated to the national interest but it has been well illustrated that the war was seen by the majority of Free Churchmen as a crusade for the survival of Christian values. Shakespeare merely copied this communication to the "Secretary of each denomination outside the Church of England and the Roman Catholic Church."[208] The general view was: how could people object to fighting, or at least supporting those that were fighting, in such a 'righteous' cause? How could Conscientious Objectors simply stand by and let German aggression and injustice succeed because they would not fight?

---

203 Ibid, p.3

204 Keith Robbins, 'Protestant Nonconformists and the Peace Question,' Ed: Alan Sell and A. R. Cross, *Protestant Nonconformity in the Twentieth Century*, Carlisle: Paternoster Press, 2003, p.225

205 Keith Robbins, 'The British Experience of Conscientious Objection,' *Facing Armageddon: The First World War Experience*, South Yorkshire: Pen & Sword, 2003, p.693

206 *BT*, 14th January 1916

207 'UB Minutes,' 5th April 1918, p.105

208 Ibid, p.105

G. H. Laslett C.F.(U.B.) some insight into how chaplains were used to question soldiers who refused to fight for reasons of conscience in an article entitled 'The Conscientious Objector and the Unconscious Hero.' This article gives a detailed account of a discussion he had with such a soldier who was even refusing to polish his buttons, do up his tunic and pay the common courtesy of saluting a commissioned officer.[209] It is interesting to note that Laslett refers to himself as having objections to war and when asked how he can then serve answered: "As the result of a simple sum in moral proportion. Great as is my conscientious objection to war, my objection to oppression is greater, and greater still is my conscientious objection to let other men fight for me whilst I procured by the sacrifice and do nothing for them."[210] It is from this viewpoint that Laslett courteously questions this religious soldier's position and suggests that: "If Christ were here, do you think He would be sitting at ease enjoying the comforts procured by the sacrifice and pain of others? No; I think He would be in the trenches helping our brothers."[211] This conversation reveals how they believed that the war effort was a Christian duty.

In spite of this view Free Churchmen did seek to defend the Conscientious Objector's rights, especially after the conscription rules were put into place in 1916. This is understandable because most Conscientious Objectors if they "were religious, as many of them were, they usually hailed from one of the nonconformist churches such as the Baptists, the Methodists or the Quakers rather than from the Church of England..."[212] The law now placed those who had conscientious objections to the war in direct conflict with the British State. They could no longer just 'not volunteer' but had to argue against being called up. Those who steadfastly refused military service had to stand before a 'Tribunal' to seek exception. These Tribunals became platforms for presenting their arguments for by "definition, conscientious objectors were articulate and eager to discuss and debate. This eagerness came often from their up bringing within the independent Free Churches. Most Conscientious Objectors were content to accept alternative non-combatant service but about 1,500 were considered to be "absolutist" and a number of these were "subjected to brutal punishment."[213] Up to 34 Conscientious Objectors, for example, were forcibly deployed on military service in France and

[209] G. H. Laslett, 'The Conscientious Objector and the Unconscious Hero,' *BT*, November 10th 1916, p.687
[210] Ibid, p.687
[211] Ibid, p.688
[212] Will Ellsworth-Jones, *We Will Not Fight: The Untold Story of World War One's Conscientious Objectors*, (London: Aurum Press Ltd, 2008), p.8
[213] Randall, 'Conscientious Objectors,' p.14

were "sentenced to death for refusing to obey military orders."[214] Shakespeare was a defender of the individual's right to object to the war without suffering persecution or cruelty.

The next chapter will focus primarily on Army Chaplains for the simple reason that the Royal Air Force (R.A.F.) was not yet in existence and the first U.B. Royal Navy Chaplain, David Merrick Walker, although commissioned in 1916, would remain shore based until 1920. The U.B. chaplains would be chosen carefully for chaplaincy service at the Front because of their qualities. The war gave an unprecedented 'opportunity' for evangelism and other Free Church 'Pioneer Work.' They were to be the spear head of their denominations' expansionism and that of the expected revival, but how would they minister at the 'Front'; at the 'Base Camp and in the 'Convalescence Camp' and would it be effective?

---

[214] Ibid, p.15

Chapter Three

The United Board on Active Service

I. Into the Firing Line

The Great War was to cost the lives of millions in the trenches of Belgium, France, Macedonia and Turkey. Life would become brutal and expendable. When Robert Graves, a serving soldier of the Great War, answered the question, what was life like in the trenches? He wrote:

> Our homes, our privies, our graveyards; like air-raid shelters dug in a muddy field, fenced by a tangle of rusty wire, surrounded by enormous craters, subjected not only to an incessant air-raid of varying intensity, but to constant surprise attacks by professional killers, and without any protection against flooding in times of rain. And the smells: of corpses, latrine buckets, rotting sandbags, human sweat, chloride of lime, frying bacon. And the sounds; clatter of working parties, rattle of dixie-lids, squeak of rats; laughter and curses and, at sunrise and sunset the cry of 'Stand-to.'[215]

But nothing seemed as terrifying as an artillery barrage. Dubrulle, serving during the battle of Verdun, summarises such a barrage in a few sentences and helps us to grasp something of the absolute horror, and constant stress and strain, for those serving in the front line. He wrote:

> When one heard the whistle in the distance, one's whole body contracted to resist the too excessively potent vibrations of the explosion, and at each repetition it was a new attack, a new fatigue, a new suffering. Under this regime, the most solid nerves cannot exist for long... perhaps the best comparison is that of seasickness.... finally one abandons one's self to it, one has no longer even the strength to cover oneself with one's pack as protection against splinters, and one scarcely still has the strength to pray to God.[216]

T. N. Tattersall described in detail an experience which took place at the beginning of the First Somme offensive in 1916. He uses strong biblical imagery

---

[215] *The Sunday Times*, 9th November 1958

[216] Jay Winter & Blaine Baggett, *1914 - 1918 The Great War and the Shaping of the20th Century* (London: B.B.C. Books, 1996), p.167

which allows us to enter the mind of Tattersall and helps give us a clear impression of what it was like for those serving at the Front and for their chaplains serving with them. He explains that: "Dawn opened with the song of birds. I listened to their hymn of praise with an intensity of feeling never known by me before... Thinking filled me with sorry and leaden-eyed despairs. Thousands of men, with limbs a-quiver and loud-beating hearts, were waiting not far away for the signal to engage in battle."

At 0500hrs the bombardment of German lines began and it "seemed as if ten thousand demons of hell had been let loose in an ungovernable rage." This bombardment and the strain of waiting to attack took its toll on a number of soldiers. Tattersall described how a few "broke down," suffering amnesia, loss of reason or the loss of speech.[217] E. L. Watson confesses "that shell fire did not try my nerves as severely as the cracks of the rifle followed by the ping of the bullet that reminded one of the fact that an enemy's eye was constantly waiting for a good sight of you. Shells come by chance to the individual, but these bullets by deliberate aim."[218]

At 0600hrs the allied attack began and Tattersall committed himself to working with the Regimental Aid Post. Following the battles he would spend time with those suffering from light wounds doing "what little [he] could to help." He would then visit the more seriously wounded at the Advanced Dressing Station. Once he had visited the wounded he would visit the troops at the 'Reserve Trenches' and then move to the rear to visit the Gun Batteries, returning again to the 'Advanced Dressing Stations'. During this work Tattersall saw many sights that he wished he could forget. The stress and strain for all concerned must have been severe and by the afternoon, it had become unbearable for some. Tattersall remembered sharing tea in a dug out when "a stretcher bearer broke down into tears, unnerved by the awful sights and sounds."[219] Tattersall found it hard to present effectively the sheer horror of war, although he was certainly graphic. He explained that it "would be impossible to give an adequate account of the appalling condition of things when the battle rages with hellish ferocity. But let not the people at home forget that even on the quietest day losses are suffered and precious lives are laid down for our country's honour and salvation."[220] He then reports that two hundred casualties would be expected on a 'quiet day.' Fisher explains what he did after a major offensive. He says that "We find out our own lads, take their home addresses and their Christian names, so that we can send word to their folk,

[217] Spurr, *Chaplains in Khaki,* p.65
[218] W. E. Watson, 'Our Baptist Chaplains in France,' *BT,* December 4th1914, p.880
[219] Ibid, pp.67-68
[220] T. N. Tattersall, 'Collecting the Sick and Wounded,' *BT,* August 6th 1915, p.515

distribute the ever-welcome cigarette, comfort those who are in pain, pray with those whose time is short, or chat with those who sit awaiting their turn, and listen to their stories."[221]

The Gallipoli Campaign[222] on the Turkish Peninsula, where British, Australian and New Zealand soldiers and their chaplains served, was similar. In nine months of fighting the "casualty figures were appalling: ...the Australians lost 8,709 men killed, the British 21,255, the French 9,874, the New Zealanders 2,701 and the Indians 7,594. A staggering 86,692 Turks lost their lives defending their homeland."[223] W. Dexter, an Australian chaplain, describes the aftermath of a Turkish attack in gruesome detail. He records in his diary that:

> The ground was simply covered with dead between the trenches at various points and after the day's work of burying estimates [of] up to 12,000 Turks killed have been made. It was simply awful... Amongst this awful mass of dead Turks were some of our own boys who had been killed on the 1st and 2nd days' fight and had lain there since. Many of our missing could now be classed as dead. The bodies were horrible to look at being black and swelled up stretching out the clothing and in many cases when they were touched falling to pieces.[224]

These were the new and terrible surroundings in which U.B. chaplains found themselves in which they had the challenge of presenting the good news of Jesus Christ, not in a respectable pulpit but within the context of total war, a war that would undermine all the certainties of previous generations. John Wolffe notes the struggle that 'Christian' British Society had with past theological certainties while having to deal with the common scenes of horror that this war created. "When unburied bodies had to be left to rot in no man's land and human flesh and bones protruding in macabre fashion from the ground and from the sides of trenches, glib teaching about the Resurrection could not be readily assimilated."[225] The Christian influence on Western European countries, such as Great Britain and Germany, cannot be understated. Most of those serving in the trenches, on both sides, had been brought up within the church and Sunday School and so it was possible for Merrick Walker, who was serving troops as a O.C.F. at a home base in Scotland,

---

[221] Fisher, *Khaki Vignettes*, p.74

[222] It was the Allied attempt at an amphibious invasion of Western Turkey in 1915 and 1916. See Pope & Wheal, *Dictionary*, pp.181-186

[223] Michael McKernon, *Padre: Australian Chaplains in Gallipoli and France,* (Sydney: Allen & Unwin 1986), p.39

[224] Ibid, p. 85

[225] John Wolffe, *God and Greater Britain Religion and National Life in Britain and Ireland 1843 - 1945*, (London: Routledge, 1994), p.241

to presume that a group of soldiers whom he had just met had come from active Christian backgrounds. He asked "You are all old Sunday School boys, I suppose?" They replied with a resounding "Yes, Sir."[226] In the *Christian World* an incident is described that confirms the impact of the Christian influence on those serving at the 'Front.'

> Were you the minister who prayed by my bedside last week?" the sick man asked. The United Board Chaplain had not been in that particular ward for a fortnight. "A minister came," the man continued in broken speech, "When I was too ill to move or speak. He knelt by my bed and prayed and the prayer helped me. I should like to thank him." The chaplain wished it was him who had been so honoured – but it was another. The wounded sergeant could only speak in gasps because he had been shot in the lungs.
>
> During his subsequent visits, the Chaplain heard the story. The Sgt, was a backslider who, after attending a Mission as a young boy and youth in the midlands had stopped going and hadn't been near a church for seven years. On a mission to take and hold a hill the Sgt. had been shot by a German sniper. One of his colleagues, a Scotsman called Sandy, suggested he (the Sgt.) prayed. The British had to pull back, leaving the Sgt. behind. The Sgt passed out and the next faces he saw were Germans. One of them kicked him and laughed, saying the Sgt would do harm. (At least that's what the Sgt. thought he said). He passed out again and came round as the British started shelling the hill. He remembered Sandy's suggestion and his heart gushed with prayer. "God bless my little children. God bless my wife. Save me." The shelling began to quieten and the Sgt. started saying, "Father, Father – You would never believe how I felt. That's when I found God." Then the shelling started again, but this time it was German. The Sgt. started to crawl back towards his own lines when he was found by Sandy and a party of stretcher-bearers. "Was it not wonderful how I started to say 'Father'"? "Yes brother it was" replied the chaplain, "A voice came to you. It has the same voice that once called 'Saul, Saul' on the Damascus Road."[227]

A. M. Perkins in his book entitled *Between Battles* written in 1918 described a moving scene that took place while waiting for the train at a "Siding one wet Sunday night" during the battle of Passchendale (autumn 1917).[228] These wet and

[226] *The United Navy and Army Board Serving the Soldiers and Sailors*, p.119

[227] 'Sandy's Suggestion,' *Christian World*, January 3rd 1918

[228] "Passchendale. Popular name for the Third Battle of YPRES, a contemporary byword for useless slaughter derived from the name of the ridge that was the last objective taken by the offensive on 6

tired men "began to sing, and it was not 'Tipperary' but 'Lead, Kindly Light...' Then followed 'Rock of Ages' and other well-known hymns... The eyes of the Y.M.C.A workers were filled with tears as the voices of men going into battle rang out:

The night is dark, and I am far from home,
Lead Thou me on."[229]

Obviously such events show that many soldiers were heavily influenced by the Church, whether Established or Free. Tattersall related another story, indicating the pervasive Christian influence upon the average soldier, about a soldier who asked his friend, Pte J. Downs, a Welsh Baptist, to "tell my wife I am ready, that to God I have given my trust."[230] Soon after he was shot in the head and died. During the Ypres Offensive a soldier wrote a little letter that would help comfort his family if he was to fall in battle, and this is another example of the all pervasive influence of the Christian faith. He writes: "To my darling wife and children. Daddy fully surrendered to Jesus 20.11.14 at Ypres. Sudden death - sudden glory. Safe in the arms of Jesus."[231] It is well documented that formal Christianity was the major religious influence on the soldiers serving at the Front, but denominational allegiance became less important as the war went on. Tattersall suggests that as early as 1914, the "soldier's religion is not of the 'pious' order, and sentimentality does not touch him. He has little or no interest in denominational differences and theological problems."[232]

The religion at the Front was, generally, guided not by denominational allegiance but by whether the chaplain spoke of Christ in a way that related to life in the trenches and was also willing to share the common experiences of trench warfare. Tattersall recognised that a common question asked by soldiers. 'Why should one man be taken and another left?' "Invariably Tommy says, 'Fate'...as though we are in the grip of a blind, remorseless, impersonal Force."[233] When Tattersall optimistically suggested 'God' the questioning soldiers agreed and therefore Tattersall believed that "providence...is their most deeply - rooted belief, and on the strength of it they go into battle."[234] Fisher concludes that the soldier's references to fate "is often their way of acknowledging a very real and simple trust

---

November 1917." Pope & Wheal, *Dictionary*, p.357

[229] A.M. Perkins, *Between Battles*, (London: T. Fisher Unwin Ltd 1918), p.50

[230] T.N. Tattersall, 'At the Base,' *BT*, December 4th 1914, p.880

[231] Sellers, *Fighting Men*, p.83

[232] T. N. Tattersall, 'At the Base,' *BT*, December 18th 1914, p.912

[233] T. N. Tattersall, 'The British Soldier in Hospital,' *BT*, April 9th 1915, p.235

[234] Ibid, p.235

in God." He explains that "One tries to put it better, of course; that we are in the hands of God, and that nothing can come to us but His own will. But I have found that it is often the same thing expressed differently."[235]

However it was not only the message that mattered: the chaplain needed personally to relate the good news to these new realities. The language that had furnished the soldiers' vocabulary was gained through Sunday School and the Church services, but the gap between this language and their new experience was growing. They wanted faith without dressing, Christ without myth and experience without dogma. In the words of E. L. Watson C.F.(U.B.): "Life is very real to every man on the field and the essentials only count."[236] Watson, because of these challenges, calls upon his fellows at home to "pray much for the boy in camp and in the inferno of the trenches that he [the soldier] may prove true to the training of home and chapel."[237] C.S. Rose C.F.(U.B.) also explains that "practical Christianity is the thing that matters. Men distinguish between 'religion' and Christianity."[238] Theology would, therefore, only be understood through their chaplain's personality and his shared experience; he needed to be "incarnational" as well as "proclamational" in approach to his chaplaincy service. In spite of these lofty sounding words this often came down to whether the chaplain was a 'good bloke' and had shared their common experiences. David Railton, a Church of England chaplain describes his own experience. "So far I have only learnt that our Englishmen do not care a pin whether a man is high or low, Broad or Catholic, or a Dissenter, whether he gives allegiance to Canterbury, Rome or General Booth. He just cares if a man is genuine."[239] For Tattersall the soldiers' "instincts are deeply rooted... There is no parade of religion in the army. A Soldier is a man of action. A doer not a sayer. He has scant respect for broad phylacteries. He looks for the proof of faith in moral heroism especially in his padre." He continues: "On a route march the soldier can see by the expression on the padre's face that a chaplain's blisters are just as sore as anyone else's... the rain is just as wet and the mud just as dirty."[240] According to Harold A. Thomas, an Anglican who shared a dugout with a Methodist and Baptist chaplain, the soldiers' conversation was rarely centred around God but, "for the most part conversation centred around one or other of two subjects, 'Beer' and 'Women', the two things without which life would not be worth living for the people who have never had the education or

[235] Fisher, *Khaki Vignettes*, p.135
[236] E. L. Watson, 'Our Baptist Chaplains at the Front,' *BT*, December 18th 1914, p.912
[237] E. L. Watson, 'A Baptist Chaplain at the Front,' *BT*, November 27th 1914, p.863
[238] C. S. Rose, 'The First Baptist and Congregational Soldiers' Institute,' *BT*, January 1st 1915, p.IV
[239] Michael Moynihan, *God on Our Side. The British Padre in World War I* (London: Secker & Warburg, 1983), p.59
[240] Ibid, p.26

opportunity to cherish any other ideals."[241] But what he describes was true not just for those who had little 'education or opportunity.' E. L. Watson writes about the growth in gambling and drunkenness, especially amongst the soldiers serving in the East. He comments that excuses are "made on account of the rougher conditions under which the men live. When the experiences of the past twelve months are remembered, one is much inclined to be lenient towards the men who have proved heroes...I love them all, though I grieve over much that could be different."[242] F. C. Spurr related that "Thomas Atkins does not wear his heart upon his sleeve and his language at times may be lurid and even repulsive"[243] Yet in spite of his perceived godlessness "Tommy believes in the Padre."[244] This was the context and ethos in which Free Church chaplains would be sent to operate in.

II. Chaplains at the Front

Charteris believed that the "influence of the Chaplain over the men depends on one thing - his obvious physical bravery." During a sermon he preached in 1941, at Ayr Baptist Church, clearly influenced by his own war time experience, Charteris declared that "Courage is not the absence of fear but the overcoming and control of fear... Courage is not one virtue amongst many but the soil in which all the Christian virtues grow. Men sometimes laugh at religion. They never laugh at courage... It is the heritage of all who have the true knowledge of God in Christ Jesus."[245] Certainly, those "who proved themselves here [Gallipoli] would find a place in the [soldiers] affection that nothing subsequently could challenge."[246] W.P. Rhodes C.F.(U.B.) believed that "[I]f a chaplain thought first of his own skin, he had better stay at home, for his duty takes him constantly amidst danger."[247] Watson described his approach succinctly in the *Baptist Times.* He said that "I simply go where I am needed most and can serve the men best - trenches, advance dressing stations, field hospitals and rest camps."[248] Thomas Howell C.F. (U.B.) was said, by his Senior Chaplain, to have "died a hero's death, having stuck to his post in his Division where he had gained the whole-hearted love and admiration of officers and men ever since arrival in France just 17 months ago."[249]

---

[241] Moynihan, *God on Our Side,* p.108
[242] E. L. Watson, 'With the Mediterranean Expeditionary Force,' *BT,* July 16th 1915, p.473
[243] Moynihan, *God on Our Side,* p.12
[244] Ibid, p.13
[245] W. C. Charteris, 'Courage,' *SBM,* 76.7, July 1941, p.5
[246] Michael McKernan, *Padre Australian Chaplains in Gallipoli and France,* (Sydney: Allen & Unwin, 1986), p.40
[247] Henry Smith, *Stories from the Front by United Methodist Chaplains,* (London: Henry Hooks 1917), p.51
[248] E. L. Watson, 'Our Baptist Chaplains in France,' (*BT,* December 4th 1914), p.880
[249] *Congregational Yearbook,* 1916, p.65

There is ample evidence that this was the model that U. B. chaplains adopted during the Great War as the following citations reveal.

Rev. George Smissen C.F.(U.B.) awarded M.C. [250]

For conspicuous gallantry and devotion to duty. He went forward with the assaulting troops to the objective and at once set to work tending the wounded and comforting the dying under very heavy shell-fire. Though badly bruised by a fragment of shell, he carried on until all the wounded had been dealt with. His cheery presence amongst the men acted as a great tonic and had an excellent steadying effect. [251]

Rev. Herbert Leggate C.F.(U.B.) awarded M.C.

For conspicuous gallantry and devotion to duty. He worked among the wounded at an aid post in an advanced position, and carried many wounded men in through a heavy barrage for a considerable distance. His splendid example gave great encouragement both to the wounded and to all those working with him[252]

Rev. Herbert Leggate C.F.(U.B.) awarded second M.C.

For conspicuous gallantry and devotion to duty at 'Sommaing on 24th October, 1918. 'Heavy casualties were incurred in the battalion from machine-gun fire. He went forward on has own initiative, and on three occasions carried in wounded men under heavy machine-gun fire. Throughout the operations during period 24th October to 1st November, 1918, he behaved admirably. [253]

Rev. William Henry Jeffries C.F.(U.B.) awarded M.C.

For conspicuous gallantry and devotion to duty. He rendered most valuable assistance in attending wounded. He conducted bearer parties, and assisted in collecting wounded. He was continuously under heavy shell fire. His conduct throughout was a fine example to all. [254]

---

[250] The 'Military Cross' was a British award for conspicuous bravery in the face of the enemy
[251] *London Gazette*, 18thOctober 1917
[252] *London Gazette*, 7th March 1918
[253] *London Gazette*, 18th October 1917
[254] *London Gazette*, 16th August 1917

Rev. William Jollans C.F.(U.B.) awarded M.C.

For conspicuous gallantry and devotion to duty. He went up with the motor ambulance cars under heavy shell and machine-gun fire, and assisted in dressing and carrying the wounded. Throughout the day he was of the greatest assistance to the R.A.M.C., whilst his cheerful courage under fire *was* most praiseworthy.[255]

Rev. Thomas William Hart C.F.(U.B.) awarded M.C.

On two occasions he has shown great devotion to duty under heavy shell fire in assisting to collect wounded. His work and assistance in attending to the wants of the wounded both in the front trenches and in the advanced dressing station have been invaluable and worthy of the highest praise. He has carried out his duties under shell fire in a cool and resolute manner.[256]

Rev. Abraham Rees Morgan C.F.(U.B.) awarded M.C.

For conspicuous gallantry and devotion to duty. He rendered the greatest service to the battalion by his organisation of stretcher bearers and dressing stations during an engagement. He showed complete contempt of danger.[257]

Rev. Alfred Thomas Morgan C.F.(U.B.) awarded M.C.

For conspicuous gallantry and devotion to duty in action. He assisted the Medical Officers day and night in tending the wounded. His cheerfulness and fine military spirit have done a great deal of good in the Brigade.

Rev. Frank John Walkey C.F.(U.B.) awarded M.C.

For conspicuous gallantry and devotion to duty. He was most untiring in his efforts throughout the day in bringing in the wounded under heavy shell fire, and his courage and perseverance inspired all ranks. On several previous occasions he has shown the greatest devotion to duty under fire.[258]

E. L. Watson also described his own experience of moving forward with his

[255] *London Gazette*, 16th September 1918
[256] *London Gazette*, 20th October 1916
[257] 4th supplement to the *London Gazette*, 2nd July 1918
[258] *London Gazette*, 24th August 1918

stretcher bearers to collect the wounded. He wrote "[on] account of the constant sweep of rifle fire by day it is impossible to remove the poor fellows until night, when the difficult and dangerous work begins. The average trench is only about two feet wide by five to seven feet deep, and carrying wounded men through these winding passages past the riflemen in pitch darkness means agony to the patients, and grave trouble to the stretcher - bearers."[259] Watson received no medal for bravery but this experience was probably normative for most chaplains who were serving at the Front. A. T. Veryard C.F.(U.B.) was killed as "He was going through the trenches occupied by his Brigade, as his custom was, cheering and preparing his men for an attack. Just before it commenced he was in a shelter speaking to some officers, when it was hit directly by a shell... he was killed... instantly."[260] John Ash C.F.(U.B.) was killed similarly when a German aeroplane dropped a bomb directly onto his billet while attached to the 48th Ammunition Column on 7th September 1917.[261] William Jollans C.F.(U.B.) was awarded an M.C. "for swimming across a river three times with the wounded after a bridge had been blown up"[262] while serving with the 34th Division.

Another U.B. Chaplain of special interest is the 24 year old W. E. Jones C.F.(U.B.) serving with the 2nd Royal Welsh Fusilers, who also served at the Front. Captain J. C. Dunn, the Regimental Doctor recorded Jones' presence on a patrol in his memoirs for June 1918: "When it was time [for the patrol] to return... the Germans started traversing machine-gun fire along our line. In the labour and risks of getting casualties 'over the skyline and through the wire as day was breaking...' a young Non-conformist padre, called Jones stood in the gap in the wire directing the party which way to go."[263] Later referring to his untimely death on the 8th October 1918 just outside of Villers Outreaux, Dunn records that "Griffiths, an outstandingly good officer, was killed, as was our Nonconformist padre. The padre should not have gone with A Coy in the early morning. He was told he would be an embarrassment to them; but he was impulsive, he insisted on going, and was killed when seeking an M.C. to please some fool of a girl in Liverpool who had taunted him with having no decoration."[264] It is equally plausible to believe that Jones had a desire to demonstrate that the recently recognised U.B. chaplains were as good as any other chaplains. It was also a fundamental belief of the more dynamic chaplains such as Studdart Kennedy and Charteris that soldiers would only give the chaplain a hearing if his 'courage' was

[259] E. L. Watson, 'With Our Baptist Chaplains in France,' p.880
[260] 'The Death of the Rev. A.T. Veryard CF,' (*BT*, July 6th 1917), p.415
[261] John Ash CF WO339/126157
[262] *Daily Express*, (17th February 1933), p.15
[263] J. C. Dunn, *The War the Infantry Knew 1914-1919*, (London :Abacus, 1994), pp.489-490
[264] Ibid, p.556

beyond question. Ieuan Elfryn Jones, a Ph.D. student at the University of Wales, Bangor has translated letters and articles held in the files of the Baptist Union of Wales which have revealed the high regard in which Jones was held and because of the controversy surrounding his death it is worth quoting from them in detail. James Evans, the 122 Brigade Chaplain and the senior overseeing W. E. Jones, sent a letter to *Seren Cymru*[265] to be printed. He wrote about hearing of:

> the death of our esteemed colleague and dear brother the Revd E Evans Jones... He was hit in the head, and died soon after, whilst accompanying one of the assault companies of his battalion...The news of his death went like a shock wave through the battalion, as Mr Jones was well known throughout the Division, even though he was mainly in support of one of the Brigades... He was commonly known as the 'Baby Padre'... not just because he was the youngest one with us, but also because of our love and esteem for him... Mr Jones proved himself to be one of our most faithful, acceptable, and successful chaplains... His greatest achievements were in the sermons during his life out here, not in those in the pulpit ... and his greatest was the one we heard on the morning of Tuesday 8th October outside Villers Outreaux: And the sound was heard from afar.
>
> ...His character was very much one of a pleasant, committed and enthusiastic individual ... he was a happy and cheerful person ... He was fully committed to his studies of the Word. Although relatively inexperienced, he was always grateful for the encouragement and assistance of his colleagues in the difficult work that we have out here. On top of his preaching and pastoral duties towards the 'boys out here', he also worked hard to assist them with their welfare needs...
>
> ...During the recent battles, he had been responsible for the burial of the dead in his Brigade area. Following the battle outside Gouzancourt, where many of the Welsh Division fell, he organised the clearance of the bodies and the setting up of what he named the 'Arfon British Cemetery.'[266]

This letter revealed a very different chaplain to that portrayed by Dunn. The basic facts agree and maybe he was advised not to go on patrol, but this chaplain was committed passionately to Christ and to his soldiers. The soldiers in return deeply respected their padre as the above letter illustrates. In another letter sent by E.

[265] 'Seren Cymru' translated as 'The Welsh Star' was a Welsh language weekly newspaper of the Baptist Union of Wales

[266] Tr. Ieun Elfryn, Jones, Letter from Rev James Evans to Seren Cymru, published on 8th November 1918

Edmunds to J. Gwili Jenkins, Principal of the North Wales Baptist College, the qualities of W. E. Jones' character are again promoted. We were greatly saddened to hear of his loss, as he was an excellent young man, and one of the best workers, that we could have hoped to have with us. His Colonel reported that he went out with one of the units during the assault, and he was killed whilst ministering to the wounded during the battle"[267]

In fact Welsh Baptists seem to have seen him as someone they "had great expectations for in the future."[268]

No matter how the facts of W. E. Jones's death are reported and interpreted, this episode, and others like it demonstrate that U.B. chaplains freely elected to serve at 'the front' and share the hardships and dangers of those they were seeking to serve. Fisher demonstrates the constant dangers faced by chaplains. A fellow chaplain Hubert Spink "lay (dead) in the dust by the roadside, with half a dozen boys of his own battalion lying dead around him."[269] W. P. Rhodes C.F.(U.B.) gives us a rare in sight into how Free Church chaplains coped with the constant fear of death at every turn in the trenches. He recorded that "[w]hen I know I am going into certain danger I always definitely commit myself to God's keeping: and then, if I have an impulse to go, or not to go, here or there, I obey it as a direction of the Lord. This habit certainly saved me, at least from danger."[270] He further writes that a "chaplain's work is fraught with daily danger, but calm and confidence always come when he remembers that he abides under the Shadow of the Almighty."[271]

Less glamorous, but equally important was the work of those chaplains serving Base Camps. Rose believed that "The relationship of the camp to the 'front' has not been placed in its proper setting by the average soldier. It is really as the root to the tree, or the shop to the window. There can only be a 'front' by erecting a back. The two help to make a structure."[272]

III. Chaplains Behind the Front

Peris Williams C.F.(U.B.) a Welsh speaking chaplain and former teacher[273] was

---

[267] Tr. Ieuan Elfryn, Jones, Letter by Mr E Edmunds to Rev J Gwili Jenkins, Friday 25th October 1918

[268] Tr. Ieun Elfryn, Jones, Letter by Ifor Jones, of the North Wales Baptist College, Friday 25th October 1918

[269] Fisher, *Khaki Vignettes*, p.98

[270] Smith, *Stories from the Front*, p.55

[271] Ibid, p.56

[272] C. S. Rose, 'Institute,' p.III

[273] Peris Williams, 'Diary,' p.14

serving initially, as an officiating minister, while awaiting his army commission. He went Northampton to serve the spiritual needs of predominantly Welsh speaking soldiers. He wrote in his diary that "I came here to work for Jesus Christ among the soldiers who have come to Northampton from different parts of the country."[274] That same evening he was met by R. Parry Jones C.F.(U.B.) and they went to a Y.M.C.A. tent for a 'concert.' Williams described the scene that met him. The tent "is much bigger... than the one in Wrexham... This is undoubtedly an excellent provision... The majority of those in the tent were boys from the 7th Battalion - Welshmen from Merionethshire and Montgomeryshire."[275] The day after seeing the vast numbers he was seeking to serve Williams was plagued by self doubt. He wrote that this "morning after awaking I was uncertain that I would be of any use here to the boys. After coming down I opened the Bible and the first words that my eyes fell upon were these: 'Fear not, for I am with you, I am your God, be not dismayed: I will strengthen, I will support you, I will uphold you with my trusty hand.'"[276] He accepted this as a promise from God and entered fully into seeking to challenge and win men for Christ. He was soon involved with the Y.M.C.A. tent ministry that was held every evening and was packed with troops.[277] Services in the Y.M.C.A. tent and local church buildings were regularly used for these services. Williams described another service, this time in a Town Hall. "A good congregation assembled some 300. I began the service and Mr Parry Jones preached from Matthew 111.9. He preached well but too long... At the end...We appealed to the boys to come forward to sign the temperance pledge, and 37 came forward."[278] Often at these meetings, Williams with colleagues would seek to give out Bibles and new testaments to the departing soldiers, mostly printed in the Welsh language and supplied by the Bible Society.[279] As he writes "Hoskins and myself went to the place where a large number of the soldiers of the 6th Battalion RWF [Royal Welch Fusiliers] (men from Caernarfonshire), assemble, and we distributed about 500 Welsh Testaments."[280] The soldiers happily took the Bibles and some of their responses are recorded by Williams.

> Whilst distributing Testaments, one of the boys from Caernarfonshire told me that he had read the copy which he had received three times over since he had been here, from the Gospel of John, and that he had enjoyed it more and more each time. He took his well-worn copy from his pocket. He was

[274] Ibid, p.1
[275] Ibid, pp.2-3
[276] Ibid, p.5
[277] Ibid, pp.6-8
[278] Ibid. p.25
[279] Ibid, p.13
[280] Ibid, p.13

very proud of the Testament and said, 'I'm sure I will get much pleasure from reading this once more.'[281]

This positive response was not always the case. Williams one wet morning was giving out some of the few English versions of the New Testament when one soldier told him "that he didn't want a copy. 'I don't want one I am Church of England.' After explaining that the scriptures were the same for all the denomination the zealous young Anglican happily took one."[282] Sometimes Williams was able to use the opportunity made possible by this ministry to challenge the receiver about 'eternal things.' On one occasion, as he was bidding farewell to the RWF as they entrained for France, Williams asked a soldier if he had a Bible. The young soldier answered 'no.' "I gave him a copy and he was very glad to have it. I told him that I hoped he would return but that if he had to die, that I hoped he would die in the Lord. His eyes filled with tears and we left, perhaps, never to see one another again on this side."[283] On another occasion a wife and four children had come to the train station to say farewell to the husband and father. Williams offered some testaments and offered to pray with them. "The door was closed. We went on our knees. I delivered them to the care of our Heavenly Father; asking him to protect them, and, if in accordance with His will, prayed for them to return alive, but if they would have to die, then that they would be allowed to die in the Lord"[284] As these soldiers pulled out of the station Williams "tried to look happy, and raise their spirits."[285] In the day Williams would visit the soldiers billeted with families[286] and the wounded and dying in the local hospitals[287]

On January 26th 1915 Peris Williams was sent a letter from the War Office informing him that had been granted a commission as a chaplain[288] and would be serving in France. He then began preparing for deployment to France, but took the opportunity to return to Wales and speak about his chaplaincy work at Gyfeillach Congregational chapel.[289] Once he arrived in France he spent a day getting to know the local area and took the opportunity to visit local Roman Catholic churches which he described as 'splendid.'[290] The Day after he was met by a

[281] Ibid, pp.16-17
[282] Ibid, p.29
[283] Ibid, p.21
[284] Ibid, p.33
[285] Ibid, p.38
[286] Ibid, p.6
[287] Ibid, p.20
[288] Ibid, p.40
[289] Ibid, p.48
[290] Ibid, p.55

fellow United Board chaplain, Rice. After a short period of fellowship while staying at the Hotel Dieppe Williams was sent to give pastoral oversight to six hospitals four miles from Rouen.[291] He would give his time to visiting the soldiers and officers who had been injured at the Front and at times became very fatigued though this would not stop his impressive work.[292] His commitment to these soldiers was impressive but obviously being especially interested in Welsh speakers and would often write home for them. One morning he met a W. R. Roberts from Llanwrst[293] and wrote a letter to his mother informing her of his injuries. She wrote back thanking him and correspondence was begun. Later he visited an incoming draft of the 6th Welsh Regiment recruited from Swansea and gave them testaments, cigarettes sent by R. J. Wells, the Congregational Secretary.[294] Williams was a proactive chaplain with a strong sense of calling which enabled him to overcome fatigue and other difficulties but always had a special commitment to Welsh speakers and this often took priority over mere denominational allegiance.

F. J. H. Humphrey C.F.(U.B.) was the Free Church chaplain responsible for "shepherding Presbyterians, Methodists, Congregationalists, Baptists - in fact, all who are neither Church of England nor Roman Catholics,"[295] He also covered three military hospitals in Alexandria where there was to be "none of the joy of marching with strong healthy men, and very little respite from the presence of pain, disease and death. Much strength, physical, mental and spiritual, is needed, and none would fain make a large claim upon the ministry of intercession."[296] In an article for the *Baptist Times* Humphrey indicates to his readers that he censored his own writing. He told them: "I cannot write of the things I have seen; some are too shocking, some are too sacred. It is easier and pleasanter to record the truly magnificent devotion of doctors and nurses and the splendid patience and indomitable cheerfulness of the men."[297]

As a Base chaplain Humphrey often had the task "far too frequently, of telling men (who are so far from home and loved ones) that they must soon take the last journey." He considered that some of his most poignant experiences had been associated with the final hours of brave men.[298] Much of his work was of a more intimate and personal nature than would be common within normal Baptist

[291] Ibid, p.56
[292] Ibid, p.75
[293] Ibid, p.60
[294] Ibid, p.63
[295] F. Humphrey, 'At the Dardenelles Base,' *BT*, July 23rd 1915, p.483
[296] Ibid, p.483
[297] Ibid, p.483
[298] Ibid, p.483

ministry. Life away from the Front was difficult and had its own unique challenges. However, there were opportunities in the Base camp for a typically British[299] evangelistic service. One such service was described by Humphrey in an article for the *Baptist Times*. Humphrey travelled to the outskirts of Alexandria to a large tent where the rally was to take place. On entering he saw "a crowd of men, soldiers and sailors, with coats off and shirts open, sitting, lying, and standing, covering nearly every inch of ground."[300] As he made his way through the crowd he noticed a small group of men praying at the side of the tent. Humphrey believed that there was "power in that prayer-meeting, and I felt a bit sorry when the men got up from their knees and passed out for the service."[301] The service began and the soldiers chose the hymns they would sing, including 'when the roll is called up yonder' which was a popular choice amongst soldiers. The singing continued until it was time for Humphrey to speak. Believing "very little there is to say unless one has a Gospel to preach,"[302] that is what he proclaimed. Many of the soldiers presented before him had been recuperating from the effects of action at Galliopoli and many were returning the next day. Humphrey reported that he had never "spoken to a more responsive audience, and never, I think, have I felt a deeper sense of responsibility... [for some] would not return again. And they settled themselves to listen as men before whom the issues of life and death were sharply set, with a strained attention, and a silence that was almost too impressive."[303]Many responded and Humphrey enthusiastically declared: "A great work is going forward among the men of the Army and Navy; everywhere it seems that there is a ready hearing and acceptance of the Gospel."[304] He added that in "this horrible war men have sounded the deeps, deep has called unto deep, the deep of human need to the deep of Divine mercy."[305]

IV. The United Board and Revival

Michael Moynihan makes his assessment that the revival did not actually happen. He concludes: "From hindsight the First World War padres can be seen as spearheading a hoped-for religious revival that failed to materialise."[306] Certainly there is a lot of evidence to support this view in statements of the time. Phil J. Fisher C.F.(U.B.) stated in *Khaki Vignettes* that "I simply mean to say that those

[299]These revivalist services seem to have characterized British chaplains who were influenced, in particular, by the Welsh Revival of 1905.

[300] F. Humphrey, 'A Camp Evangelistic Service in Alexandria,' *BT*, August 27th 1915, p.559

[301] Ibid, p.559

[302] Ibid, p.559

[303] Ibid, p.559

[304] Ibid, p.559

[305] Humphrey, 'Dardanelles Base,' p.483

[306] Moynihan, *God on our Side*, p.14

who imagine that war, *qua* war, is a tremendous converting agency understand nothing at all about it. Great manifestations of a revival character may have occurred in some instances, but they have not come within the range of my knowledge."[307]

One reason often given for the failure of the expected revival was that war is destructive of all that is good. James Pollock, a Y.M.C.A chaplain serving in Flanders in 1917, when answering the question, "What about revival among the men at the front?" said:

> Not only…were there few signs of such a revival apparent, but he found it difficult to understand how any revival could be reasonably expected. What was there in war to quicken moral or spiritual life? He saw more in it to coarsen and harden. Indeed… unless there were the anti-septic of a saving idealism, the spirit of the soldier would only be debased.[308]

Tattersall also reflected that "All that we know of war is that it destroys good and increases evil."[309] A. J. Tweedie, a Church of Scotland minister, had already concluded in 1916 that the war "was heavily on the side of deterioration of human character." Tweedie remained unimpressed with reports of revival at the Front and refers to it angrily as "the spasmodic pieties of the danger zone…the conditions of war are not an evangelistic agency…"[310] David Coulter described the often unexplained reality of life in the army. He wrote: "There was little respect among the troops for the moral teachings or authority of the Churches, which was reflected in widespread petty theft, profanity, gambling, drunkeness and prostitution. The mood of 'trench fatalism' increased the understandable human need to live life to the full before it was too late."[311] Another factor that must be taken into serious consideration is that there was a great deal of prejudice against revivalist approaches to ministry. Morris Murray, a High Anglican Padre, described a Nonconformist service that he had experienced at the front. "It is a nice little dugout and at the time of my visit, full of non-conformist soldiers with whom a Welsh Padre was praying in English. He was thin and tall and wore no robes. He had that earnest Revivalist look and his voice was at once melodious and odious."[312] It is not therefore surprising, based on significant evidence, that the

---

[307] Fisher, *Khaki Vignettes*, p.133

[308] James Pollock, 'West United Free Church. Religious Aspects of YMCA work in Flanders,' *Stirling Journal and Advertiser*, December 13th 1917, p.3

[309] T. N. Tattersall, 'War and the judgement of God,' *SBM*, January 1940, p.5

[310] Cited by Coulter, 'Church of Scotland,' p.9

[311] Coulter, 'Church of Scotland,' p.10

[312] Moynihan, *God On Our Side*, p.118

"the discourse on the war came to be dominated by anti-revivalist interpretation."[313]

Recently there has been a revision of this point of view. Snape, a leading chaplaincy historian, challenges this 'anti-revivalist' interpretation: "Bluntly stated, casualty levels at Ypres, Gallipoli, Loos and the Somme were such that many of the men who experienced either a religious conversion or a deepening of their faith in 1914-15 simply did not survive or remain in the army long enough to become hardened or disillusioned."[314] It can be argued strongly that a revival at least at a local did take place and its effective failure was due to other reasons. Snape explains: "Death, wounding, transfer and reorganisation destroyed the original character of many units which had once harboured strong religious cultures. In other words, the religious revival of 1914-15, like many other smaller revivals in the British army since the 1740s, could not survive the inevitable attrition and disruption of hard and sustained campaigning."[315] Independently of Snape, after a significant study of Baptist chaplains during the Great War, I[316] came to a similar conclusion: "The smouldering glow which was all that was left of the expected flames of revival received a further dampening in the final year of the war when a flu epidemic swept through Europe killing around ten times more people than the war itself. It is obvious that many who sincerely underwent a religious conversion or were religiously revived died before they could impact church or society."[317] The debate will no doubt continue. The most balanced and pragmatic view has been expressed by T. W. Hart C.F.(U.B.) a Welsh chaplain as early as 1916. He wrote in the *Baptist Times* at the time that: "Much has been written and spoken on the bearing of the war on religion. Some affirm that it will give rise to a revival of religion, while others hope that it will, and some doubt the survival of religion as we have known it. Out here we have no time for doubting religion. We are too busy using it…" Yet he could confirm that "our boys are all seeing 'more' and deeper, and farther than ever they did before coming here, and if they are spared to return home, and if they will not be disobedient to the heavenly vision, they will be in touch with that for which the Church stands, and one hopes that the Church will be in touch with them."[318] In an article entitled 'Our Volunteer Army' John MacBeath puts it more forcibly: "Large sections of the men are profoundly interested in religous problems... The war has made faith

[313] Schweitzer, *Cross and the Trenches*, p.192
[314] Snape, *God and the British Soldier*, pp.167-168
[315] Snape, *God and the British Soldier*, pp.167-168
[316] See Neil E Allison, 'Baptist Chaplains Revivalism at the Front (1914-1918),' *BQ*, Vol:42 October 2007
[317] Allison, 'Baptist Military Chaplaincy,' p. 173
[318] T. W. Hart, 'A Chaplain in Picardy,' *BT*, October 20th 1916, pp.638-639

difficult. Some of them suffer the shock of a tragic disillusionment. But they are not satisfied with doubt. They fight their doubts." Those who make their way to faith realise that it is "Christ or nothing. And the great Captain of salvation draws in his train a new volunteer army." The services held in France bore eternal fruit and "many a deathless covenant was made; many a life was surrendered to the Saviour... The great Evangel changes for them the darkness to dawning, and the life immortal rises out of the womb of death."[319]

The spiritual climate in the trenches was as high as was morality, though amongst some it was low. There is plenty of evidence that spiritual awakenings were happening and that the spiritual strength of many was able to withstand the assaults to the senses that traumatic war brings. In the forces the U.B. chaplains had a significant part to play in these revivals. W. M. Field C.F.(U.B.) had experienced such awakened interest in Egypt. He explains that after

> a most arduous and trying day, in which I had totalled eight services and ploughed from post to post through sixteen miles of soft, yielding sand, I was sitting at my tent door before turning in, dead beat, for the heat had been unbearable, when an N.C.O. saluting me, said, 'Some men wish to speak with you, sir.' God forgive me, I thought them tiresome! Their radiant young faces were lit up with a warmth and glow that completely transfigured them, and I knew that the alter-fires within were burning brightly. 'Oh, sir,' they exclaimed, 'we've had a prayer-meeting since the service, and some of the boys have decided to start a new life... Positions were reversed. They taught me, for they had hold of a truth, and were gripping resources, Divine resources, that were still denied their padre. What was this wonderful thing, this unutterable joy that never failed them, however exhausting the day and perilous the task?... They were flooded with light just because they were possessed by God, whose indestructible Spirit defies the batteries of a continent and all the appalling conditions of modern warfare.[320]

U.B. chaplains took every opportunity that was presented to them to commend faithfully the gospel of Jesus Christ. One such opportunity was the normal worship and parade services that the army required. Tattersall held such a service regularly at the Convalescent Camp. "A hymn, a prayer - often broken with hearty Amens - a lesson, another hymn, and fifteen minute sermon on home on Country and God, another hymn, Benediction and then the National Anthem made up the order of

[319] McBeath, 'Volunteer Army,' pp.85-6
[320] Smith, *Stories from the Front*, pp.90-91

our service, which generally lasts about three-quarters of an hour. Then a little personal conversation with the men as they trooped out."[321] L.G. Hughes C.F.(U.B.) described a very similar service. He records that the "ordinary length of the parade service is thirty-five minutes from start to finish-bright singing, a short lesson, a *multum-in-parvo* prayer, and a brief straight, manly talk."[322] A. E. Bray C.F.(U.B.) tells of a service that came about through an introduction to a Commanding Officer who requested his help in organising a service for his men. The Commanding Officer gave him "such a cordial reception and was so hearty in making suggestions for the success of the service, that [Bray] felt [he] had better tell him I was a Free Church padre. 'Don't matter a bit,' he replied. 'Give us a service and some of the hymns we can sing, and I shall be most grateful.'"[323] So it was that Bray had the joy of preaching to six hundred officers and other ranks who sat on the grass in a circle around him. The response to this service was enthusiastic and he was asked to come again.

At the Base Camp and during the extended lulls in the fighting, opportunities existed for chaplains to visit the hospitals and rest areas. They would also have the opportunity to present the gospel in a typically revivalist fashion, and this was often achieved through a 'Voluntary service.' "Such Voluntary services were more popular with both chaplains and soldiers than compulsory services, as they were ecclesiastical rather than military events."[324] These services would emphasis a strong call for the soldiers to get right with God, through Christ and his finished work, before the final judgement. Such services, which had a strong emphasis on preaching, would be followed frequently with an 'Altar Call' where those who had come to faith or wished to rededicate their lives would show their earnestness by raising their hands or by coming forward to the 'altar.'

E. L. Watson was to have an extremely effective ministry using such voluntary services, although his "one regret is that I have not been able to remain long in personal touch with the men who have decided for the Master."[325] He would take every opportunity to hold such services in whatever form was convenient. He made no use of prayer books or ritual, nor did he ever read his sermons. But he always spoke from the heart, using stories and illustrations in abundance and making frequent use of the 'Altar Call.' F. C. Spurr speaks of Watson's immense popularity with the troops and presents a detailed description of Watson's approach to public ministry and also its effect. Watson himself believed that

---

321 Spurr, *Chaplains in Khaki*, p.59
322 L.G. Hughes, 'A Chaplain's Sunday in France,' *BT*, July 30th 1915, p.499
323 A. E Bray, 'A Service at the Front,' *BT*, June 4th 1915, p.363
324 Robinson, 'Role,' p.37
325 E. L. Watson, 'With the Mediterranean Expeditionary Force,' *BT*, April 21st 1916, p.243

"Voluntary services depend solely upon the love and respect of the men for the chaplain."[326] Watson was popular with the troops. George Kendall, a Primitive Methodist chaplain, confirms this. In an article entitled 'The Revival at the Front' Kendall reported: "You can always be sure of a crowded parade when Captain Watson is announced to conduct it."[327] At these services Watson preached robustly and with burning clarity of "the Saviour, of His wonderful love, of His power to save...*and*...pleads with them earnestly to dedicate their lives to His Service."[328] Watson reported that the men "only want the truth that grips and heals."[329] On one occasion one hundred and thirty men made public declarations of faith and fifty the next night. In one week two hundred and twenty eight men made decisions at these 'voluntary' services. Numbers could be judged effectively because of Watson's follow-up method. After any public service Watson would call his hearers to make a decision for Christ which was then recorded on a slip of paper, giving their name, address, rank and regiment. Watson's records never asked a person's denominational allegiance. The reason is possibly because Watson was only interested in a person's personal faith which could be expressed within any Christian denomination. In a letter printed in the *Baptist Times* Watson comments:

> My Sunday voluntary services are an increasing joy to me; and many are the rich tokens of God's presence. Narrow bigotry is pressed by the few, but not tolerated by the great majority. The men care little what a man professes: it is really what he is that counts, be he of one creed or another. denominationalism to some is even unknown... The great need most deeply felt by the bulk out here is the conscious presence of God.[330]

These kinds of services were conducted without the normal denominational trappings "in all sorts of buildings and under all kinds of conditions, in order to reach the men."[331] George Kendall C.F.(U.B.) describes a 'voluntary' service held in a Y.M.C.A hut, which had "a large platform" and was situated within a Convalescent Camp. The building was filled to capacity, and after the soldiers favourite hymns were sung, Watson spoke on the text, "I, if I be lifted up from the earth, will draw all men unto me." Kendall describes Watson's effect, "With burning eloquence he speaks of the Saviour, of His wonderful love, of His power to save, and the men love 'the old, old story'... He pleads with them earnestly to dedicate their lives to His service. 'One hundred and thirty men,' he says, 'made

---

326 Ibid, p.243
327 George Kendall, 'The Revival at the Front,' *BT*, July 9th 1915, p.453
328 Spurr, *Chaplains in Khaki*, p.71
329 E. L. Watson, 'Laughter and Tears at the Front,' *BT*, February 19th 1915, p.115
330 Ibid, p.115
331 E. L. Watson, 'Our Baptist Chaplains at the Front,' *BT*, December 18th 1914, p.912

the great surrender last Sunday evening in another camp. How many will record their vows to-night, and begin a larger and more hopeful life?'" Kendall reckoned that fifty responded and "gave their lives to the Saviour's keeping. And so in two camps at this base the work of grace has begun."[332] After a few more hymns were sung Watson addressed the audience again, illustrating "his message with stories that grip. Stories from the battlefield, from personal experiences, from the lives of great men."[333] Again he appealed for them to give their lives to Christ and forty eight responded "and so in one week 228 men have made the 'great acceptance.'"[334] It is clear there was an enthusiastic response to the gospel. Even at the Front, just behind the lines, there was a response, though Watson's approach was very different. On one occasion Watson "found the men eagerly waiting for the service," which was to be held in a barn not far from the front line so no singing was allowed. During this brief service, 'somewhere in France,' Psalm twenty-seven was read, the Lord's Prayer was said, and intercessions for the "wife and kids" were made. Then Watson gave a "few heart to heart words and our service was over."[335]

W. C. Charteris describes a similar volunteer service that he was able to lead. Eight to nine hundred Welsh troops turned up to the service having walked through a gale force wind and torrential rain. The service was likened to an 'Evans Roberts' revival meeting with soldiers praying and weeping in repentance before God. Unusually at such a revival meeting, the Lord's Supper followed, though Charteris had difficulty serving the elements around the 'tables,'[336] possibly using the 'compact set' requested in 1915.[337] Charteris led a number of such services, often attracting hundreds of soldiers whether the service was situated in the 'Home Front,' the 'Base Camp' or just behind the front line. At the conclusion of another service held at the home front in the Y.M.C.A. hut in Wareham "about 100 men raised their hands for Christ..."[338] Another service at the home front was described in some detail by Charteris. He explained that the "first night he (Mr. W. R. Lane) told the story of his conversion in his own inimitable way, and at the close fully a score of men professed faith in Christ. The second night fully one hundred men raised their hands as a sign of decision to serve Jesus ... The following night Mr Kennedy (of Boscombe), who was wounded at the front, told of his experiences as a Chaplain in the field. He gave a very solemn address and made an earnest

[332] Kendall, 'Revival,' p.453
[333] Ibid, p.453
[334] Ibid, p.453
[335] Watson, 'Our Baptist,' p.912
[336] W. C. Charteris, *SBM*, 43.4, April 1917, p.58
[337] W. C. Charteris, *SBM*, 41.1, January 1915, p.12
[338] W. C. Charteris, 'Letter to Mr Walker,' *SBM*, 41.1, January 1915

appeal to the men to 'trust in God.'"[339] Christmas gave another opportunity for Charteris to commend the faith. On one "Saturday night... the room was packed with men...Welshmen gave fine zest to the singing...It reminded me of the days I spent in Wales during the Evan Roberts revival meetings. We had the Lord's Supper at the close, every man remaining to share the holy feast....As one after another poured out their heart's desire in prayer, strong, brave men were moved to tears."[340]

It is worth noting Charteris' use of Holy Communion in these voluntary services, to symbolize the soldiers' commitment to Christ and Christ's commitment to them. This was Charteris' Christ-centred 'Altar Call,' for "Personal religion," he observed, "is more potent and vital."[341]

Charteris had a great hope for a Christ-centred revival, with the Great War acting as the catalyst. This belief is communicated in a letter Charteris wrote to A. T. Walker. In a new sector of the line, "somewhere in France," Charteris is eager to record "two special features of our work here. The Wesleyan chaplain and I conducted a voluntary evening service, and had the hall packed each night. So many remained to the after-service that we could not deal with them all... I also conducted a Wednesday evening fellowship service and this steadily increased till our room could scarcely hold the men who came." Despite the shelling which at one point he describes as "merciless" he wrote, "We were very sorry when the order came to remove, because we felt that we were on the eve of a great awakening." However, he recognized that "all things work together for good to those who love Him" and Charteris remained hopeful and ended his narrative with a request to "Please go on and pray that God will give us a great revival."[342] His constant prayer was for people to come to Christ. On another occasion Charteris wrote: "The men here are just splendid, but the work is great and the task difficult, so we covet your prayers. Many have the veil taken from their eyes and they see beauty in Christ. Many have discovered and rediscovered the great cardinal truths of our religion, and find great comfort in the glorious Gospel of the Grace of God."[343] On another occasion Charteris wrote:

> The Wesleyan chaplain and I conducted a voluntary evening service, and had the hall packed each night. So many remained to the after service that we could not deal with them all. The men required to be in their billets by a

---

[339] Spurr, *Chaplains in Khaki*, p.127
[340] Charteris, 'Wayside in Flanders, ' p.58
[341] W. C. Charteris, *SBM*, 41.9, September 1915, p.156
[342] W. C. Charteris, *SBM*, 42.6, June 1916, p.91
[343] W.C. Charteris, 'By the Wayside in Flanders,' *SBM*, 42.4, April 1916, p.58

> certain hour. I also conducted a Wednesday evening fellowship service, and this steadily increased till our room could scarcely hold the men who came. We were very sorry when the order came to remove, because we felt that we were on the eve of a great awakening. But these things are in God's hands - 'all things work together for good to them who love Him' - so we go on hoping yet to gather more fruit. Please go on and pray that God will give us a great revival.[344]

Charteris believed that he was to "minister to the spiritual needs of officers and men, therefore the record of his work is the record of a Gospel ministry, the story of conversions."[345] He further declared that "the duties of the padre are manifold, and his methods vary, but his one business is to preach the Gospel... He never lacks a welcome for this message. Where else can the soldier find strength for his hazardous calling or comfort in suffering and death."[346]
The expected revival may not have materialised in a way U.B. military chaplains had hoped but they were effective in bringing many hundreds of soldiers to Christ before they entered a Christ-less eternity.

> War may not have brought about a far-reaching or general revival, that would have a social impact, but they rejoiced that God's ability to draw men to himself was not hindered by war... Certainly... chaplains were satisfied with their revivalist work during the war even if society did not benefit from a religious and social resurgence. Although their work did not produce a flourishing transformation on earth, they were satisfied it had brought about a great harvest in eternity.[347]

When revival services became less possible nearer to the 'Front' the chaplains had to minister the faith through a quiet word here and there as opportunities arose. E. L. Watson wrote: "My Sunday parades are very broken now we are on active service. My men are scattered over a wide area, consequently all service rendered now has to be of a personal character. Reaching fewer, I gain more, and am wonderfully encouraged in my task."[348]

---

[344] W.C. Charteris, 'From One of Our Chaplains,' *SBM*, 42.6, June 1916, p.91
[345] W. C. Charteris, 'The Army Chaplain on Active Service,' *SBM*, 40.10, October 1914, p.158
[346] W.C. Charteris, 'Forwarning the Church: Army Chaplain's Straight Talk,' *SBM*, 42.12, December 1916, p.187
[347] Allison, 'Baptist Military Chaplaincy,' p.220
[348] Watson, 'A Baptist at the Front,' p.863

V. The 'Quiet Word.'

Not all the work of the chaplains was in public ministry; most of the work would be achieved with a quiet word, a simple prayer or a kind act. Fisher reflects:

> So our work is done in the trenches. Services are impossible there, of course, where to gather a number of lads together might mean a tragic sequel; but one can meet them and have a little talk, which is worth much in cheer to them and in reactive blessing to oneself. There, where death is face to face, hearts are unlocked, and unforgettable impressions may be produced, though few words pass between... it is the time when fellowship means most, and the comforts of God become most real.[349]

Sometimes in the trenches the words expressed were of the most basic kind. J. Penry Davey C.F.(U.B.) writes of this. "Our talk... was necessarily short and to the point. Often the Chaplain would simply in passing say, "Cheer oh, lads," and the answer would be "Cheer oh, sir." Sometimes he would stop and have a few words with the men who were resting, and in leaving say, "God bless you; take care of yourselves, boys.""[350]

Charteris' reveals the importance and sensitivity of this approach when offering pastoral care for the dying: "A wounded captain was hit by shell fragments in the back. I arrived he was conscious for a minute, and after a brief prayer I could only sit and hold his hand. In his delirium he talked to his men so nicely, charging them to take the greatest care... Soon afterwards he passed to his home and reward."[351] Burials were obviously a constant activity for chaplains serving in the Great War and because of the freedom in being a Free Church chaplain they were able to hone the burial service in a way they found relevant. Sydney Jones commented that the "elasticity of the Free Churches enables a chaplain to use other than the stereotyped words of committal; and believing as I do, in the sanctity of the service that the soldier is rendering, I try to recognise the exceptional significance of fidelity to death in this war by using these words of committal: 'Seeing that this son of our Empire, this servant of our nation, this soldier of the King, has fallen in battle, we therefore commit his body to the grave, &c.'"[352]

One patient facing death asked Thomas Jones C.F.(U.B.) to teach him to pray. Another asked about forgiveness. Having talked about vital matters "immediately

---

[349] Fisher, *Khaki Vignettes*, p57

[350] Smith, *Stories from the Front*, p.124

[351] W.C. Charteris, 'From One of Our Chaplains,' *SBM*, 42.6, June 1916, p.91

[352] S. Jones, 'Honouring the Fallen,' *BT*, October 5th 1917, p.599

he burst into tears and said 'I do want forgiveness'... His pale face let up with new joy and hope as he listened to me, and as I paused for a moment he exclaimed, 'how beautiful! It's just beautiful and so simple why didn't I believe that before?'"[353] From the same article Jones relates another of his experiences of personal work:

> There are times when visiting hospital that a message would be brought asking me to visit some serious case. One afternoon I was asked to see a young fellow nineteen years of age. In a few minutes I was at his side and soon learned a few facts concerning him, his home and church. As he lay there pale and worn, with features as delicate as a young girl's he told me about his father and said, 'My dad is a good fellow in a way, well meaning enough - but - you know, sir?' Yes, I guessed his meaning. Then with a smile of supreme satisfaction he said, 'But my mother! Oh, sir, she is an angel,' and for a moment he turned his face from me that I might not see the tears which filled his eyes. How I wished that mother could have heard her dying boy's description of her. Then he asked, 'Will you give me a drink, sir, please?' The nurse heard the request and would have served him, but, 'No, I want the chaplain to do it. These nurses they are a tease, sir, there's no living with them,' he remarked with a playful smile. I got the water and kneeling at his bedside as I served him I asked if he knew who it was said, 'If any man thirst let him come unto Me and drink'? 'Yes, sir, it was Jesus,' and there was music in his utterance of the name 'Jesus.' We dwelt on the subject for a moment or two, and I was satisfied he had tasted of the Water of Life. Three days later I buried him in the military cemetery.[354]

While Tattersall was engaged in his visiting rounds he would give out cigarettes, food and clothing donated by the Baptist Women's League. He gave these gifts for their own sake, "to help those who might again face the rigours of war," although he also recognised that they afforded him an opportunity to help these soldiers "realise more vividly Gods' gift. On one occasion he describes how he made these gifts his text "to point them to the love which is over and about them."[355] Often a "warm wrap, a piece of carpet... or a hot drink to a sick man, were the keys with which hearts and ears were opened to the gospel."[356] Thomas Jones described similar experiences while serving in Gallipoli during the "great battles" of August. During this time Jones spent much of his time at the hospital near the rest camp,

---

[353] Jones, 'Warpath in Gallipoli,' p.191
[354] Ibid, p.191
[355] Spurr, *Chaplains in Khaki*, p.151
[356] 'The United Army and Navy Board,' p.118

visiting and giving out cigarettes to the wounded. Like Tattersall he was sent supplies of sweets, cigarettes and warm clothing from home and being the "only Chaplain in the neighbourhood"[357] Thomas Jones took charge of all the funerals. While visiting the hospital Jones engaged soldiers in conversations about their lives and would then introduce spiritual issues such as prayer, forgiveness and faith. He was obviously popular as large numbers sought to attend his services to sing and hear the gospel message. Yet U.B. chaplains were happy to show kindness for its own sake; "Having attended to one wounded man on the landing pier I asked him if there was anything more I could do for him, 'No, sir, thank you, but I should like a cigarette,' he replied. My supply had run out, but looking round I saw a young pier hand smoking and asked him for one, which I lighted and gave to the wounded man, who thanked me and said, 'This makes all the difference, sir.'[358]

James Hair, while relating his previous experience as a Y.M.C.A. chaplain during this Great War, listed the secular activities which are provided for the troops. He finished his article describing a practical job he got involved with. He said that the "Lantern and even cinematograph were also enlisted to lend interest and variety. If all this seems to some people lacking in the distinctively Christian element, I would commend to them a re-reading of the Parable of the Good Samaritan. To us it seemed a truly Christian form of service to provide for our fighting men a home from home."[359] However this kind of ministry was not without personal cost as Donald Maclean related in article in the *Baptist Times*. He wrote about his work which was mainly visiting the sick and wounded, he also described the effect on him. He wrote that "We look around the ward. But it does not do to look too long. There are nights when one goes to bed, but instead of sleep comes a nightmare of writhing, pain-racked bodies, maimed arms waving in the air, and heads and limbs swathed in bloody bandages. And that is no good for anybody."[360] Similarly G. E. Minnear C.F.(U.B.) following the Somme Offensive of 1916 wrote that "I thought I should drop off to sleep quickly after such a busy day, but I cannot. I am haunted with a vision of that battlefield... Some of the poor old boys will probably be lying there in shell holes half buried and unconscious, with their life's blood slowly oozing out."[361] Minnear, was also disturbed by the thought of those "killed and buried at the same moment, and my heart aches for those at home who may never be able to find the spot where the bodies of their dear ones lie. I see, as I have seen before, the mangled remains of splendid fellows lying around in various

---

[357] T. Jones, 'Warpath in Gallipoli,' p.190
[358] Ibid, p.191
[359] James Hair, 'The Scottish Baptist Hut,' *SBM*, 75.10, October 1940, p.9
[360] Donald Maclean, 'The Mornings Work Concluded,' *BT*, September 7th 1917, p.543
[361] Smith, *Stories from the Front*, p.27

attitudes."[362] Yet he consoles himself with the knowledge that "[t]heir spirits have gone to the God who gave them, and their names are written on His 'roll of honour.'"[363]

Clearly, in spite of their personal struggles, Free Church chaplains were using every opportunity to share the good news of Jesus Christ and 'win souls' for him. There was a clear expectation that God would indeed bring a 'revival' even as these soldiers faced the reality of life and death in the trenches. Certainly, Tattersall "carried to [his] bed the message of a bright-faced, though wounded soldier, 'This war has brought me nearer to God.'"[364] As Fredrick Humphrey made clear that there was no hesitation in speaking of "sin and atonement and salvation."[365]

[362] Ibid, p.27
[363] Ibid, p.28
[364] T. N. Tattersall, 'The Day of Battle,' *BT*, May 28th 1915, p.347
[365] 'At a Military Depot in Mesopotamia,' *BT*, November 9th 1917, p.676

Chapter Four

Experiential Theology

I. United Board Chaplains reflections on Communion

The priority of Holy Communion was being rediscovered in the trenches of the Great War and this was reflected amongst Free Church chaplains. Certainly, it was acknowledged that "Roman Catholic chaplains appear to have been particularly successful, perhaps because their administration of the Sacraments gave them a well-defined and comforting role among frightened, suffering and dying men."[366] This "Catholic model of frequent sacramental worship became increasingly popular with soldiers of all denominations"[367] and the Anglo Catholic position within the Church of England gained support for their practice of reserving the sacrament and praying for the dead.[368] Wilkinson in *The Church of England & the First World War* explains: "In situations that are totally new and bewildering, rituals can supply boundaries and sign posts, so reducing the sense of chaotic novelty."[369] William Ewing, a Church of Scotland chaplain serving in Gallipoli, certainly saw its value. He wrote that "[t]he men down from the front seemed specially to value it, and our tent was often quite full. There was a peculiar solemnity and impressiveness about these Communion services with men many of whom had narrowly escaped death, and would go forth on the morrow to face it again. The fellowship of the Holy Table yields a certain tranquillity and strength to the hearts of men who lack not courage, but to whom the long-drawn conflict brings weariness."[370]

Thomas Jones described a moving communion service that he led while he was serving as chaplain during the fateful Gallipoli campaign. He recounts the following experience:

> Services are not easily arranged on the peninsula, as being constantly within range of shell fire, the congregating of large companies of men is too risky. Still, we managed to hold services and at times if well sheltered there with large numbers attending and all show interest in singing and in the Gospel message. One Sunday evening recently our gathering was not

---

[366] Ibid, p.241

[367] Robinson, 'Role,' p.39

[368] Ibid, p.46

[369] Wilkinson, *Church of England*, p.133

[370] William Ewing, *From Gallipoli to Baghdad*, (London: Hodder & Stoughton, 1917), p.128

more than 150, but all felt the presence of the Prince of Peace in spite of such tumult of war. At the close we distributed several gifts from Scotland, and every recipient was most grateful. Then the Lord's Supper was observed, and a season of real spiritual blessing experienced, as under the beams of the pale cold moon on the shore of the Aegean Sea we remembered Him who laid down His life for His friends, and we prayed for loved ones far away in the homeland, for our comrades in battle, and for ourselves. There was something very impressive in the sight of those brave fellows, as with bowed heads they remembered their Lord's death, perhaps for the last time on earth.[371]

These war experienced chaplains had developed a greater emphasis on the practice of Holy Communion. Sellers referred to this liberating change. He states that in "the Free Churches of England it [communion] has been held, as a rule, monthly, and at the close of a preaching service. At the Front we find that it is no longer confined to stated times, and is not habitually in association with preaching services. Any time and any place suffices. The great thing is 'to do this in memory of our Lord's death' as frequently as possible."[372] This could take place literally, whether in a "quiet dell, in deep dug - out, in uncomfortable barn, or in the open with the shrapnel shells bursting around - anywhere and everywhere men gather to celebrate the Lord's death."[373] W. H. Jeffries C.F.(U.B.) shares his experience of a field service just before a major offensive at the end of which Communion was offered. "To my surprise," Jeffries records, "and almost overpowering joy everyone, officers and men, stayed for Communion. We had formed a circle of three rings. My white cloth with the cup and plate glistening in the sun was in the centre. I never felt so much the solemnity and yet the joy of that most sacred of all our services...there was a very real sense of the nearness of God. It proved to be the last opportunity for Communion before going into action... Before the next Sabbath many of those present had passed into the calm of Eternal Day."[374] Fisher says that "How touchingly appreciative they are of the little service we had last Sunday... and the Communion of the Lord's Table of which we partook together!"[375] Communion was taking on a special significance. It was clearly the chaplains' desire to seal their fellowship with their soldiers and with Christ by often celebrating this intimate act of faith; for both officers and men were keen to celebrate communion before returning to the front line trenches.[376]

---

[371] T. Jones, 'Warpath in Gallipoli,' p.191
[372] Sellers, *Heroes in Khaki*, p.53
[373] Ibid, p.54
[374] Smith, *Stories from the Front*, pp.15-18
[375] Fisher, *Khaki Vignettes*, p.56
[376] Charteris, 'Our Chaplains,' p.155

John Macbeath shared that he cherished "the memory of many happy hours, great friendships, countless confidential chats; most hallowed of all were the occasions of Holy Communion, and the manifest conversion of some who became good soldiers of Jesus Christ." [377] Merrick Walker, working as an officiating chaplain at this time, details how a soldier came to a personal faith in Christ and "then asked about partaking of the Lord's Supper - to him an evident sealing of the Covenant just made between his Saviour and his soul."[378] Whether one was brought up in the church or not, in the realities of war it no longer mattered.

> Many of those who gathered round the Lord's Table with me on a Sunday evening have passed beyond the margin of our years. For some of them it was the first and last time. Their names are on my own covenant roll, and later in the casualty column, and forever in the Lamb's Book of life. In these services in France many a deathless covenant was made; many a life was surrendered to the Saviour.[379]

Sellers believed the importance of communion amongst soldiers was possibly because chaplains at the Front who took Communion were reminded of Christ's sacrifice for sin by "the thought of *their* sacrifice."[380] This was also a common understanding of communion even amongst Roman Catholic chaplains. Henry C. Day, a Roman Catholic chaplain, for example, wrote in *A Cavalry Chaplain* about a Communion service that most of his soldiers received while awaiting orders to join the Gallipoli Campaign. He declared "How much we needed it. How much it meant-Light, Life, Love, Immortality, Sacrifice... O Christ! Glorify Thy Name. Strengthen these boys. Enhance their lowliness with heroic purpose. Sanctify their lives, ennoble their deaths. Thy Will be done!"[381]

At the home front the same openness towards communion was also beginning to be expressed. MacBeath recalls that "Never can I forget the thrill of preaching to a Hut filled with soldiers - at what time the guns barked not so many miles away - and at the close holding a Communion service for these, the greater part of the congregation, who remained. The cups were ordinary Y.M.C.A. mugs, the plates were those used in the ordinary work of the Hut, the bread and wine were such as we could find; but the proceedings were in the deepest sense of the word sacramental, and the Host was as truly present as in any church or chapel. The

[377] John MacBeath, 'Scottish Baptist Churches Hut,' *SBM*, 75.7, July 1940, p.11
[378] 'The United Army and Navy Board,' p.119
[379] MacBeath, 'Volunteer Army,' p.85
[380] Sellers, *Heroes in Khaki*, p.54
[381] Henry C. Day, *A Cavalry Chaplain*, (London: Heath Cranton Ltd, 1922), pp.118-119

elements were taken round by soldiers, who in the home churches were elders or deacons. To men so soon to be at grips with death that service must have been memorable indeed."[382] At least one U.B. chaplain asked for some "communion plate", referring to a "Common Cup" and single "Plate." "I wonder if any good friend of the Church would present me with a set of communion plate? It would require to be very compact. I would like to meet all my men, at the force station, round the Lord's Table, before leaving for France."[383] In practice the act of communion was being freed from denominational narrowness to become a "Christ like" event in itself, as Sellers recalls, "Ecclesiastical labels disappear at the Front."[384] An unknown U.B. Chaplain wrote to Shakespeare describing such a communion service. "Communion at the Front is a pathetically simple thing... A lad asked me to hear confession, and when we commenced several devoutly crossed themselves as they took bread and wine. Life out here is too big for fine distinctions, and men never ask if the communion is according to the order of their Church, but simply desire to meet their Lord... We are one out here. What God has joined together let no man put asunder."[385] This incident was clearly held up as a good example by Shakespeare who had it published in the *Scottish Baptist Magazine.* It was but one demonstration of his growing vision for a national ecumenical church.

This concept, of the 'real presence' of Christ with his 'gathered people,' without reference to denominational allegiance, was being realised at the Front. A. F. Anderson, a Y.M.C.A. chaplain describes a communion service, which to his mind was unique, because "a minister of the United Free Church of Scotland administered the Sacrament, a minister of the Established Church of Scotland took round the bread, and a clergyman of the Church of England took round the wine. There was no jarring note and no disharmony."[386] The psychological and spiritual power of communion was even, at times, experienced through their enemies. One chaplain was called to minister spiritual aid to a German P.O.W who was dying. "The German was very wishful to receive the Lord's Supper, and it made no difference to him that it would be administered by an enemy's hand... To him they were all one in Christ. So...[they] took the Lord's Supper together, rejoicing in a common brotherhood. Two days later the German prisoner passed home to God."[387] This ecumenical, and even international, theology was being practiced at the Front, by conservative evangelicals, as was commonly being reported at the

---

[382] MacBeath, 'Scottish Baptist Hut,' p.9
[383] W. C. Charteris, 'Letter to Mr Walker,' *SBM,* 41.1, January 1915, p.12
[384] Sellers, *Heroes in Khaki*, p.54
[385] Anonymous, 'A Soldier's Communion,' *SBM,* 42.9, September 1916
[386] William E. Sellers, *With Our Heroes in Khaki*, (London: RTS, 1917), p.55
[387] Ibid, p.56

time, and is well documented. Certainly, the "story of these Communion services is surely one of the most interesting in the war."[388]

II. United Board Chaplains Ecumenical Experience

John A. Newton wrote that; "Granted the traditional dissidence of Dissent, it might be thought that Protestant Nonconformists would have found it hard to come to terms with the ecumenical movement of the twentieth century."[389] However, Free Church chaplains were discovering and practising a new openness which put the emphasis on the individual's needs rather than strict denominational practice and adherence. It was not always easy, for some of their Anglican colleagues continued to demonstrate a rigidity towards ecclesiastical practice, despite the heartbreaking grief it could cause. David Raw, in his biography of Theodore Hardy V.C, an Anglican chaplain, relates this story: "A devout Scottish soldier serving in an English Regiment wrote home from the front to say that he was about to take part in an attack, but he had been refused communion by the Anglican Padre. The soldier was killed in the attack."[390] C. L. Perry C.F.(U.B.) while on leave from the 'Front' spoke frankly, to an interested audience, about the sectarian attitude "being thrust by certain Anglican chaplains. They had, he said, 19 chaplains in one division, and all were working harmoniously together until a Bishop came along and told them this unity must stop..."[391] This kind of denominational bigotry was not the official Anglican position, as the Chaplain General made very clear in an interview with the *Daily Chronicle.* Taylor Smith gave the direction that if absolutely needed then a fellow Protestant could take Communion for, say, Anglican communicants, if an Anglican minister was not available.[392] This kind of 'bigotry,' therefore, must be considered an exception. Certainly, most U.B. chaplains spoke of extremely good relations with those of other denominations, including Anglicans and Roman Catholics.

Fisher wrote with deep sadness about the destruction of a small Roman Catholic Church which he reflected in eulogy. He wrote:

> O little church, there is no more sanctuary within your walls; your poor, gay flowers mark but the memorial of a shrine. Your slender spire no

---

[388] Ibid, p.55

[389] John A. Newton, 'Protestant Nonconformists and Ecumenism,' Ed: Alan Sell and A. R. Cross, (*Protestant Nonconformity in the Twentieth Century*, Carlisle: Paternoster, 2003), p.357

[390] David Raw, *"It's Only Me" A life the Reverend Theodore Bayley Hardy VC DSO MC 1863-1918* (Carlisle: Frank Peters Publishing 1988), p.17

[391] *CW*, 3rd February 1916, p.3

[392] See Sellers, *Fighting Men*, pp.46-47

longer symbolises the chant of sacred praise rising to heaven; it is but a mark by which German guns may 'register.' Your alter is piled now not with prayer, but with the dust of your ruin; your censers are cold, the fragrance of your incense is departed, usurped by the reek of powder and the acrid fumes of poisonous death. Yet, little church, I tread reverently amongst your rubble, for, broken as you are, you bear your witness, you memorialise a gracious past. Nay, I accept the token of your poor scarlet *immortelles*; there yet clings to you that which is defiant of death; there shall be a day of resurrection, and your shrines shall again be hallowed by the resurgent aspiration of man."[393]

Padre Wilkinson C.F.(U.B.) could also feel sad at the destruction of a Roman Catholic Church. He writes that "The form of doctrine taught within its walls was not mine, but I could not view the wanton destruction of that noble pile without a feeling of passionate regret."[394] Later he had the opportunity to walk around the fire-disfigured sanctuary and saw on the outer wall "a crucifix, with the figure of the Saviour that remained untouched and unscathed. Fit symbol of the things which endure! And the Saviour's face seemed to look down in sorrow on the scene of ruin."[395] Not surprisingly, the great parable teller, E. L. Watson, commented: "Every lonely crucifix by the roadside reminds one of the neglected cross in the affairs of men."[396] The crucifix became a symbol of 'sacrifice,' and depending on view point could be interpreted as a picture of hope, if one believed in the resurrection, or a portrayal of hopelessness, which soldiers began to feel as the war continued. Protestant and Roman Catholic alike could relate to this vivid portrayal of Christ, unlike the statues of Mary that many Protestants found offensive. Tattersall represented this view point. He wrote: "The Protestant is perplexed. The Name that is above names meets him not. The place the Son should occupy has been given to His mother."[397] Yet he recognised that the:

men in khaki, be they Protestant or Roman Catholic, are not unmindful of the shrines and crucifixes that abound in Flanders. The war fills our minds with dark images and fearful horrors, and we have to wrestle not only against flesh and blood, but against principalities and powers, and any reminder of things spiritual, any call back of wayward thoughts, any incentive to personal prayer is received with gratitude. Some of the shrines are very tawdry, some of the crucifixes have been broken down,

---

393 Fisher, *Khaki Vignettes*, pp.49-50

394 Wilkinson, 'Perils Oft,' p.583

395 Ibid, p.583

396 E. L. Watson, 'A Baptist Chaplain at the Front,' *BT*, November 27th 1914, p.863

397 T. N. Tattersall, 'Religion at the Front,' *BT*, June 25th 1915, p.412

but we have a great feeling of respect for the piety that erected them.[398]

As a Free Churchman he could declare that "I am of the Protestant Faith, and between me and the scarlet woman is a great gulf fixed, but I like to look upon that crucifix." [399]

Tattersall, who once said that "nothing can make a good Baptist into an Anglican"[400] could still relate that there "were some other chaplains on board, three Anglicans, two Presbyterians, and one Roman Catholic, but all denominational differences seemed to disappear in the presence of a common need and common task. They were 'Christians', not Churchmen."[401] Another U.B. chaplain (likely to be Albert E. Bray) shared his experience of the helpfulness of a Roman Catholic colleague:

> One of the Free Church chaplains speaks of an incident which occurred at _____ . He was enquiring about some of his boys when a Roman Catholic priest, fresh complexioned, and hearty, came forward and in a lovely Irish brogue he said: 'Can I be of service to ye to show ye where your boys are? I know lots of Baptists and Congregationalists and others. Away we went, and from that day I have not wanted a friend. In the hospital as we look at the men's discs, the Padre will say "Bray, here's one of yours." He came over a distance of five miles to tell me a Baptist Boy had been killed by a shell, and would I come and bury him.[402]

E. L. Watson explains the common practice amongst chaplains with regard to their denominational work, which would explain the Catholic Priest's action.

> In the rush of work a chaplain has little time to inquire *re* denomination; he gives his help where most needed; he comes as a brother man and affords God's own consolation. In the event of a burial, of course, the chaplain of the denomination to which the poor fellow belonged arranges for and conducts the service. As far as possible, each chaplain ministers to his own dying, but every man of us cares for the wounded and sick.[403]

---

[398] Ibid, p.412
[399] Ibid, p.412
[400] Tattersall, 'At the Base,' p.II
[401] *BT*, October 9th 1914, p.761
[402] Spurr, *Chaplains in Khaki*, p.19; see also *The Cross on the Sword*, p.106 and Bray, 'A Service at the Front,' p.363
[403] Watson, 'At the Front,' p.I

F. C. Humphrey illustrates how caring for the sick and dying could have significant ecumenical implications. Sellers reports that Humphrey was suddenly awoken from asleep by the 'medical orderly officer' who said "I want you to come and see a man who is dying. He is Church of England, but I don't think that matters. Be quick, or you will be too late." Naturally, Humphrey threw on a coat and went to the dying soldier's bedside and "prayed with him and did what he could to help him to peaceful end." Humphrey then returned to bed and fell swiftly to sleep only to be awoken again by an orderly who informed Humphrey that the "doctor told me to call you, sir; there is a man dying. He is a Roman Catholic, but the doctor said, 'Send for Father Humphrey, he'll do.'... That night he represented three 'religions' rolled into one- the English Free Church, the Church of England, and the Roman Catholic."[404] Sellers comments: "It was a quick transformation from the Rev. F. C. Humphrey of the United Board into Father Humphrey of the Roman Catholic Church! ... It is satisfactory that both Church of England and Roman Catholic chaplains thanked him next day for what he had done for their lads."[405] This kind of experience was not unusual at the 'Front' and could at times even transcend religion. For example during the Gallipoli Campaign a Roman "Catholic was able to comfort a dying Jew with the most generalised version of religious sentiment."[406]

Charteris' ecumenical spirit can be well illustrated by his natural acceptance of his Roman Catholic colleague as a fellow Christian and minister. "On our journey up [to the Front] our conversation had been of the wonderful leadings of God in our own lives. We both suffered from shell shock for a month, but now quite recovered."[407] He expands on this incident and writes about visiting the 'fire trenches' and the billets along with the Roman Catholic Padre while on the way to the Chaplains' Mess. After passing the 'old town' they overtook some support wagons and gained a lift. Not five minutes later "a shell burst just behind us, splintering the timber in the wagon ...We were covered in fine yellow powder, but thank God, we were not wounded... Another of God's eye winks...We both suffered from shell shock for about a month."[408] Whilst in the above mentioned Chaplains' Mess Charteris describes the warm relationship which he and his fellow padres enjoyed: "I am writing this little note from the Chaplains' Mess in a quaint little town of the West frontier. We - the chaplains - have a very comfortable mess near divisional headquarters - 4 Church of England, 2 Roman

404 Sellers, *Heroes in Khaki*, pp.172-173
405 Ibid, p.173
406 McKernon, *Padre*, p.133
407 Charteris, 'Wayside in Flanders,' p.58
408 W. C. Charteris, 'A Baptist Chaplain Mistaken for a Spy or a Funeral at Dead of Night,' *RAChD Journal*, Vol.24, No.128, December 1977, p.28

Catholic, 1 Presbyterian, 1 Wesleyan, and 1 Baptist, all reside together and I venture to say that there is no happier mess in the country. We live together and work together and help each other in the heartiest manner. We have over 30 units in the division, scattered over a very large area, and our days are spent visiting these scattered camps. In the church room at headquarters we have the Communion service at 7.30, evensong at 6.30 and family prayer at 7. Nearly every day we have to go forward and bury some of our brave fellows who have given their lives in the cause of freedom and righteousness."[409] A Roman Catholic Chaplain speaking of the same group comments:

> Those... men represented several denominations, yet no stranger suddenly appearing in their midst could have determined, by any outward and visible sign, the denomination to which each belonged. Anglican, Presbyterian, United Board, Wesleyan and Catholic - they are dressed alike; for the most part they hold common rank; they confer together, they pray together, they work together. They respect each other, although some of them profoundly differ from each other. When the war is over and khaki is discarded in favour of ordinary clerical costume, they may, and probably will, unless a miracle occurs (which may God grant), renew their differences quite openly. But never again can they be *quite* the same men as they were before the war.[410]

There was a new openness to working closely with the other denominations represented within the A.Ch.D. but it did not stop there. These chaplains also co-operated with their colleagues, with the exception of the Roman Catholics, during the many public services of worship. Charteris wrote that we "meet weekly for the purpose of arranging our services for the following Sunday... and our services in 'Orders' bear no denominational label. Often we share and also exchange services. An Anglican will preach this week where the Baptist preaches next. Last Sunday I preached in two places where the devotions were led by the Anglican Chaplain. It was an unusual experience for me, but I greatly enjoyed it... To have an Anglican service at nine, a Presbyterian service at ten, and a Baptist service at eleven in one camp would make the enemy scoff. We must unite our forces that we may do more and greater work. And our union in service will be more effectual in winning the soldier for Christ...'division would be a sin.' We all agreed. War compelled us to work together. Will it compel the workers at home?"[411] This close working relationship was not just a minority experience but was the normal practice

---

409 Charteris, 'From the Chaplains,' Mess, p.155

410 *The Cross on the Sword*, p.106 see also Spurr, *Chaplains in Khaki*, p.10

411 Charteris, '17th Division,' p.II

amongst most chaplains.

Humphrey also spoke of the warmth of co-operation between the chaplains serving in the Dardenelles, although he is more doubtful than Charteris about the wider ecumenical relevance of such united service. He writes that there

> are four chaplains on the strength - two Church of England, one Roman Catholic, and myself. We get on very happily together, but so far as the ultimate attainment of ecclesiastical unity is concerned, I am doubtful whether we are even preparing the soil, much less sowing the seed. Of Free Church unity there is much more evidence, since I am shepherding Presbyterians, Methodists, Congregationalists, Baptists - in fact, all who are neither Church of England nor Roman Catholics.[412]

This new age of ecumenical co-operation was also reflected in the United Board Minutes as early as 1915. The U.B. decided that "in the opinion of this Board, steps should be taken to secure facilities for United Board Services in Catholic churches where such buildings are available."[413] J. C. Carlile certainly had no qualms about entering a Roman Catholic Church, or even about attending a Roman Catholic service while on active service. He wrote about his experience in an article for the *Baptist Times* entitled 'Sunday in a War Zone' which was printed in the same year and he informs his readers that "I went to a Catholic service this morning, just to pray with my brothers who express their faith in another way. At this advance base things are possible, even natural, that would require a great deal of explanation at home. It was simple and devout."[414] Carlile reflects about this experience and wonders how "curious it is here. The things one has regarded as necessary have no place in the war zone - they are not even thought about. Differences at home, wide as the gulf that no man can pass over, here are non-existent."[415] Fisher concludes similarly, but more positively, that

> My experiences as an Army Chaplain have revealed much to me of the unity of the Spirit, and confirmed all my instincts not only for Free church Federation, but for the wider fellowship of Christendom... I have found that sect or denomination is no bar to Christian unity. We have worn the same uniform, we have shared the same billet, we have worshipped in the same poor sanctuary... And I for one am not coming back to squabble with other Churches over points of difference that, beside the things we

---

[412] Humphrey, 'Dardenelles,' p.483
[413] 'UB Minutes,' 10th November 1915, p.318
[414] J. C. Carlile, 'Sunday in the War Zone,' *BT*, July 9th 1915, p.451
[415] Ibid, p.451

have witnessed out here and the work we have tried to do, pale into insignificance.[416]

Fisher refers to himself as a "Free Church Catholic… for what else is a 'United Board' chaplain?"[417] W. H. Jefferies C.F.(U.B.) evidenced the same spirit, while standing in as a medical doctor after a major offensive. He wrote:

> I talked more than a doctor would, thereby, I suppose, revealing that I was a padre, and yet I felt that was part of my ministry. I forgot for the time that I belonged to the United Board. In removing men's clothing I often noticed their discs and found that I was ministering to R.C., to C. of E., as well as Nonconformists. I was careful not to trespass. But I saw in all these wounded soldiers men who had bled for Britain. I felt that the Master Himself would never have noticed those discs. Sufficient for Him that there were men in need; I felt glad that in this ministry I could act as though they were not there. Those wounds had united us, even by blood.[418]

E.A Forbes, an Anglican chaplain, who in his book *Vermelles,* published anonymously in 1918, described very movingly how this togetherness exhibited itself in the way the war graves were organised, and reflected his hope that after the war there would be a committed desire for a real church union, nationally and internationally. Forbes describes this aspiration, commenting that there

> are nearly 1000 graves, and as French and Germans lie together on the opposite side of the road, so here Anglicans, Roman Catholics and Protestants are sleeping side by side, an augury one may hope that the War, in which they gave their lives will, if it lasts long enough and goes deep enough, result in the reunion of Christendom.[419]

---

[416] Fisher, *Khaki Vignettes*, p.137

[417] Ibid, p.61

[418] Smith, *Stories from the Front*, p.45

[419] Anonymous, *Vermelles, Notes on the Western Front by a Chaplain*, (Edinburgh: The Scottish Chronicle Press 1918), p.2

Chapter Five

Post War

I. The Post War United Board

The U. B., and the denominations it represented, had proved itself in the furnace of war. But the war was now over and the number of chaplains had to be drastically reduced. This particularly affected Free Church chaplains and therefore the U.B.'s influence. Their post war establishment was to be extremely small, as can be seen by the following statistics.

Table:1:3 "Ministering to the Forces"

POST - WAR ESTABLISHMENT FOR CHAPLAINS

RAChD	CE	RC	PRESB.	WESLEYAN	UB
1st Class	7	2	1	1	0
2nd Class	17	2	2	1	1
3rd Class	19	3	2	1	1
4th Class	24	5	3	3	1

(Source: Thomson, *Ministering*, p.19)

However, on the 16th October 1918 *The Air Force (Constitution) Act* was presented to Parliament, and on 29th November it received Royal assent as the *Air Force Act*, and on 1st April 1918 the Royal Air Force came into being.[420] The R.A.F. would need chaplains. On 4th June 1918 Shakespeare had written to Major General Paine to enquire "into the relationship of the Royal Air Force to this Board, and requesting an interview."[421] Albert Bray also intimated that "he had given considerable attention to the position as it presented itself from the United Board point of view."[422] He recommended "that the utmost care should be exercised in the selection of [chaplains]. Only the best will do, and these should have some aptitude for the social, recreational and intellectual aspects of life."[423] It

[420] Michael Armitage, *The Royal Air Force An Illustrated History*, (London: B.C.A 1993), p.27
[421] 'UB Minutes,' 5th June 1918, p.170
[422] Ibid, p.170
[423] Ibid, p.171

was also at this U.B. meeting that the title of the Board was changed to the 'United Navy, Army and Air Force Board.'[424] On 7th September 1918 Shakespeare attended a meeting to discuss chaplaincy care for those serving in the R.A.F. and it was agreed that an 'Advisory Committee' should be formed and a U.B. Principal Chaplain be appointed[425] Sydney J. Jones was nominated. F. H. Wheeler,[426] a Congregationalist, and J. Firth,[427] a Primitive Methodist, were also transferred from the Army to the R.A.F. chaplaincy although it must be acknowledged that army chaplains served with the Royal Flying Corp as army chaplains before the R.A.F. was formed. One such was F. W. Ashton, a United Methodist. Shakespeare was, naturally, chosen to represent the U.B. on this Committee. This newly formed R.A.F. Chaplaincy Service allocated the United Board three Chaplaincy places it being understood "that there would be no Assistant Principal Chaplains, and that all chaplains to the RAF would in future commence with the relative rank of Major."[428] The Establishment for R.A.F. Chaplaincy during this period was to be:

CE	1 Chaplain in Chief
	1 Deputy Chaplain in Chief
	9 Chaplains
Presb.	1 Principal Chaplain
	2 Chaplains
Wesleyan	1 Principal Chaplain
	2 Chaplains
UB	1 Principal Chaplain
	2 Chaplains
RC	1 Principal Chaplain
	3 Chaplains

(Source: 'U.B. Minutes,' September 1919, pp.902-3)

While the R.A.F. was ordering its chaplaincy department, the R.N. and denominational representatives were holding numerous meetings at the Admiralty to discuss the spiritual needs of the R.N. It was during these meetings that: "It was strongly represented that the United Board had not had the representation in the Naval Service to which it was entitled."[429] The R.N. responded by undertaking a census and came to the conclusion that this was indeed the case. In 1920, the

---

[424] Ibid, p.172
[425] 'UB Minutes,' 25th September 1918, p.263
[426] F. H. Wheeler DSO MID CF WO339/116243
[427] J. Firth MC CF see F. H. Wheeler CF WO339/116243
[428] 'UB Minutes,' September 17th 1919, p.903
[429] Thomson, *Ministering to the Forces*, p.19

Admiralty allowed the appointment of United Board commissioned chaplains to three shore establishments, but did not permitted them to go to sea. The U.B. directed A. Haig, a Congregationalist, to Chatham; J. Grierson, a Primitive Methodist, to Devonport and A. E. Bray, a Baptist, to Portsmouth Shore Bases. A. E. Bray, was transferred from the army and chosen for naval service, being posted to Portsmouth on the 2nd August.[430] Bray served at Portsmouth until his premature death in 1924 from the long term effects of being gassed in 1915.[431] After Bray's death A. Norman-Heron, his medical doctor, wrote that "he had never been in good health since he had been gassed and shell shocked in France during the war."[432] In fact, another doctor could categorically state that "I am of [the] opinion that his symptoms and fatal illness were the result of injuries received whilst on active military service."[433]

It was during this period that the 'emergency' arose in Palestine (1936-1938) and the only Free Church chaplains in this theatre of operations were John Potts, a Baptist R.A.F chaplain, and the Congregationalist, D. D. Lloyd Evans, an army chaplain. The calibre of military chaplain the U.B. was still able to provide can be illustrated in the way these two men reacted swiftly and independently to the situation. They met up without instructions or approval from the War Office or the Air Ministry and decided how to split this troubled territory between them. Lloyd was situated in "Haifa, and agreed to cover the country north of Jerusalem" and John Potts situated himself in "Ramleh… [and] agreed to cover Jerusalem and the South, including the Transjordan."[434]

During the Great War the U.B. met every other month and sometimes even monthly if occasion demanded. After the war most temporary chaplains were demobbed and the U. B. began to meet every six months. This gives a clear indication that it had changed from a proactive board under the leadership of Shakespeare, to a more responsive board under the leadership of the Baptist, M. E. Aubrey (who followed Shakespeare as General Secretary of the Baptist Union) and the Congregationalist, Sidney Barry. A significant change in the denominational make up of the U.B. occurred in 1932 when the Primitive Methodists and the United Methodists left the U.B. on the 1st October 1932 to join up with more established 'Wesleyan Navy, Army and Air Force Board.'[435] In the light of these changes the U.B. unanimously proposed that an "endeavour should

---

[430] WO339/45198 A. E. Bray, O.B.E.
[431] Ibid, *Proceedings of a Medical Board*
[432] Ibid
[433] Ibid
[434] Thomson. *Ministering to the Forces*, p.26
[435] Ibid, p.20

be made to formulate plans for the establishment of a single Chaplaincy Board, to include all Free Church denominations"[436] and that this should be called 'The United Churches Chaplaincy Service.'[437] Ultimately it was decided to keep the two boards separate because of insurmountable administrative difficulties. On 21st March 1932 the Wesleyan Board met to discuss the U.B. proposal and recorded that "the Board regrets its inability to recommend the proposal of the United Board for an officially recognised Free Church Chaplaincy, both in the matter of one chaplaincy list and in the matter of officially handing over the pastoral care of its members and adherents to ministers of other Churches, when the services of its own ministers are available."[438] At a meeting of the United Board, on 15th December 1937, W. R. Marsh's proposal that the name United Board was too comprehensive now that the Methodists had left was defeated. It was decided at this meeting to keep the name as it was well established within the R.A.Ch.D.[439] H. J. Creedy, on behalf of the War Office had written that during "the Great War and the difficult period of reconstruction following it, the United Board has rendered most valuable service, not only in facilitating the provision of religious ministrations to the troops of the four denominations, but also by its advice and assistance to the Council in all matters concerning the moral and spiritual welfare of the Army generally."[440] But the U.B. was beginning to lose its strong and persuasive influence. It was generally recognised, however, that the U.B. still had an important job to do. It would not gain major influence within the R.A.Ch.D until the Second World War. As early as the end of 1939 the U.B. had recruited thirty six Baptist and thirty five Congregationalist chaplains for war service.

II. Changes in the R.A.Ch.D

On 22nd February 1919 the A.Ch.D. was honoured for its excellent war time work by being given the 'Royal' title and permitted to place this title in front of the Departmental name, becoming the Royal Army Chaplain's Department (R.A.Ch.D.). A number of organisational changes followed, the key change being the forming of a new united Protestant chaplains' department in 1920. This placed the Protestant wing of the R.A.Ch.D. under the direction of the Chaplain General. The Roman Catholics remained separate, choosing to answer directly to the War Office via the office of the Principal Roman Catholic Chaplain - also known as the

---

[436] Ibid, p.21
[437] Ibid, p.22
[438] Ibid, p.23
[439] United Board Minutes 15th December 1937
[440] Thomson, *Ministering to the Forces*, p.25

Vicar General - and thus they continued to be administered independently."[441]

On April 25th 1925, the Chaplain General, Bishop Taylor Smith, retired and A. C. E. Jarvis took over the reigns of leadership. Jarvis was also an Evangelical Anglican who had been heavily influenced by Taylor Smith, his mentor. Jarvis had served as a chaplain in the Great War and had been awarded the Military Cross and made a Companion of the Most Distinguished Order of St. Michael and St. George. Jarvis`s main focus was, according to Wilkinson, to bring the R.A.Ch.D. into an even closer relationship with the State rather than the church.

> The interwar years were a difficult period for the R.A.Ch.D, for although they were honoured by the crown for their wartime work, the churches interest in their work waned, and the pacifist movement capitalised on bellicose statements made by chaplains and senior Anglican clergy during the Great War.[442]

It would be no less difficult for the U.B. Because of the reduction of their chaplains and service men and because of being less involved directly with their chaplains after the Anglican/Protestant branches of the R.A.Ch.D. had been united, the U.B. lost significance.

All these organisational changes were occurring in a more secular post war Britain. Brian Talbot explained that:

> There had always been a significant number of people, a majority of the population, who did not attend church on a Sunday but such individuals had broadly speaking, in former years, gone along with the observance of the Sabbath. Now in the post-war era increasing numbers of them no longer felt any sense of obligation to continue that practice.[443]

Bishop William Ward reflected on this more secular world and came to the conclusion that:

> in general we may say that the most important religious effect of the war was to produce throughout mankind a new habit of mind. Whereas hitherto the majority had looked at least nominally beyond space and time offer for its incentives and rewards, now the outlook became frankly this-

---

[441] Thomson, *Ministering to the Forces*, p.19
[442] Robinson, 'Role,' p.51
[443] Brian R. Talbot, *Standing on the Rock A History of Stirling Baptist Church 1805-2005*, (Stirling: Stirling Baptist Church, 2005), p.93

worldly. Man himself, rather than his gods, became the measure of all things.[444]

Yet lessons had been learned from the war-time ecumenical experience where greater emphasis was being put on liturgies which had provided security during a time of traumatic upheaval. This was especially challenging for those in the Free Churches.

III. The National Day of Prayer Controversy

The Archbishop of Canterbury designated 16th March 1930 as a National Day of Prayer for persecuted Christians within the Soviet Union. The Free Churches supported this national call to prayer as did the Roman Catholic Church, although they decided another date was more helpful to them. This call to prayer would be a great source of controversy but would also raise an important issue of how far the authority of the State could be applied to the churches. The government's response to the Archbishop's Call to Prayer was to ban chaplains, while serving in the forces, from praying publicly about the Soviet Union because it was considered undue interference in another state's affairs. The Army council ratified the government's wishes on the 27th February 1930, when the following directive was given: "In view of the political character the controversy has assumed, that it is undesirable that intercessory prayers for Russian subjects should be read at religious services."[445] The nation's churches saw this as undue interference in things spiritual by the state and responded swiftly and aggressively to make their views known. In response, the orders were clarified to refer to compulsory church parades only and not voluntary ones. This did little to satisfy the churches and so it was further clarified, on 11th March 1930, that Military chaplains could lead such prayers outside of barracks but not within the Garrison church.

M. E. Aubrey, the then secretary of the U.B. wrote to the Secretary of State for War on the 3rd March 1930 about the call of prayer. He said:

> It appears, on the face of it, to be a regrettable interference with the liberty of the Chaplains in their spiritual ministrations and with their duty to bring home to those in their charge the recognition of the rule of Almighty God in all human affairs... I protest respectfully but strongly against the course of action adopted. It is a most dangerous precedent.[446]

---

[444] Moynihan, *God on our Side*, p.18
[445] Robinson, 'Role,' p. 67
[446] Ibid, p.67

On 4th March 1930 the *Daily Telegraph* picked up the issue and questioned whether the government was betraying the agreement with the Archbishop of Canterbury to allow chaplains to answer primarily to the sending churches concerning matters ecclesiastical. On the 17th March Aubrey continued with the debate writing directly to the Prime Minister. He wrote:

> In the *Army List* it is laid down that in their religious ministrations Chaplains are under the oversight only of the representatives of their denominations on the Interdenominational Advisory Committee. A great many of our ministers hold pacifist views and it is difficult to secure young men for Chaplaincies not because the work does not attract them, but because they dislike being, as they put it, 'within the military machine.' We have previously been able to assure them that, whilst holding the King's Commission they are under Army discipline so far as the decision of their sphere of service goes and in regard to their conduct as officers and gentlemen, but that, so far as their religious ministrations are concerned it is definitely laid down that no one has any right to interfere with them except the appointed representatives of their denominations on the Advisory Committee. That has always enabled us to get over our difficulties. But now the action of the Government seems to have entirely changed the situation... I wish to make it perfectly clear that the prayers objected to having been for Russian subjects is really only incidental."[447]

In November 1930 a meeting of the I.A.C. was arranged and the government re-stated the principle of the sending churches' right to direct their chaplains in ecclesiastical affairs. However, in spite of the churches 'victory' the pacifist movement would use this whole issue as an example of how the secular powers prevented the true ministry of the gospel, and how chaplains were mere instruments of the state. Their argument was: "The chaplain was subject to official control and therefore prevented from preaching the true principles of Christianity."[448] Snape understands that "the concept of military chaplaincy has (at best) been viewed as an embarrassing aberration and (at worst) as a blatant and even blasphemous travesty of the gospel of peace."[449] Obviously, this is a weak argument in the light of the strong reaction of the churches and the U.B., which represented serving chaplains, against this undue interference by the State. The integrity of the Free Church chaplain was preserved but the issue of Church and State relations would continue to be significant.

---

[447] Ibid, p.68
[448] Ibid, p.69
[449] Michael Snape, *God and the British Soldier*, p.85

IV. Peace and Remembrance

After the Great War there was an overwhelming desire for peace and a growing "revulsion against war"[450] and a growing interest in pacifism. "Each year, as people gathered round the memorials to those who had died in the 'war to end war', many vowed that never again should lives be sacrificed in warfare."[451] Many rejected the old declaration that it is a noble to die for ones country, 'Dulce et Decorum est pro patria mori.' Those returning from the war "saw 'Honour,' 'Courage,' Patriotism…[had] led to cruelty, lying, and blood-lust on a scale so gigantic that the foundations of civilisation were threatened."[452] Quaker playwright, Laurence Housman collated *War Letters of Fallen Englishmen*. It was in the introduction of this book that Housman wrote:

> The Cenotaph is a silent memorial of those it stands for. These letters are a memorial that speaks, and that speaks truth. And though they speak of willingness and courage, and devotion, poured out with a generosity and a faith that put to shame the feeble efforts we have made since then for the restoration of world-peace, they speak also of disillusion and doubt, and a growing distrust of war as an instrument for bringing to pass any good commensurate with so huge a sacrifice of body and of soul.[453]

The United Board chaplains had served their country well but not without significant loses. Those that perished during or soon after the Great War were:

Ash, John (U.M.)
Ashton, F. W. (U.M.)
Burns, Joseph D. [C]
Bray, Albert (B)
Edwards, Evan [C]
Fraser, Donald (B)
Hardy, J. H. [C]
Heading, W. H. (B)
Howell, T. [C]
Jones, W.E. (B)
Tomkins, W. H. (B)
Veryard, A. T. (B)
Onslow-Carleton, William [C]

---

[450] Wilkinson, *Dissent or Conform?*, p.85
[451] Gwilym O. Griffith, 'Absolute Pacifism,' *BQ*, Vol. 9, No.8, October 1939, p.85
[452] Ibid, p.87
[453] Cited by Wilkinson, *Dissent or Conform?*, p.86

Powley, Walter (S.A.)
Raine, F. (U.M.)
Wood, H. W. (B)

Seven of these were killed in action; three died of wounds received on active service; four died of influenza, one in an accident and one suicide. Some like W. E. Jones were easy to classify. Jones was serving with the 2nd Royal Welsh Fusiliers and died while on patrol attending the wounded. Dunn records that "[w]hen it was time [for the patrol] to return... the Germans started traversing machine-gun fire along our line. In the labour and risks of getting casualties 'over the skyline and through the wire as day was breaking...' a young Non-conformist padre, called Jones stood in the gap in the wire directing the party which way to go"[454] when he was killed. Others like William Onslow-Carlton were less clear cut. He did not technically die as a serving chaplain but was killed in action in October 1918, three months after relinquishing his commission. Onslow-Carlton was returning home to South Africa on the Japanese liner 'Hirano Maru,' when it "was torpedoed off the coast of Ireland."[455] Also Albert Bray served as an army chaplain but was transferred to the navy. He was posted to Portsmouth on the 2nd August 1920[456] and there he remained until his premature death in 1924 from the long term effects of being gassed in 1915.[457] Bray's doctor could categorically state that "I am of [the] opinion that his symptoms and fatal illness were the result of injuries received whilst on active military service"[458] with the army. The influenza pandemic also took its toll.[459] Evan Roberts reported for duty to Number 3 Officers Training School at Tidworth and died two weeks later. Similarly William Heading reported to the same school and died a week later. Two others, Walter Powley and E. Edwards also died of influenza. A particularly tragic death was that of Foster Raine who was found hanging in a train at North Road Station and the coroner's verdict was that he had taken his own life.[460] The United Methodist minutes simply, but movingly recorded that "... darkness came and took his gentle, manly spirit from us..."[461] The A.Ch.D. Memorial in the Royal Garrison Church at Aldershot includes the names listed except Bray; Heading; Edwards and Ashton.[462] These deaths do not reflect the greater number of

[454] Dunn, *The War the Infantry Knew*, pp.489-490
[455] Peter J. Howson, 'Deaths Among Army Chaplains 1914-1920,' (*Journal of the Society for Army Historical Research*, Vol. 83, No.333, Spring 2005), pp.4-5
[456] WO339/45198 A. E. Bray, O.B.E.
[457] Ibid, *Proceedings of a Medical Board*
[458] Ibid
[459] Howson, 'Deaths Among Army Chaplains 1914-1920,' p.17
[460] See *Daily News*, (9th & 12th December 1918)
[461] *The Story of the United Methodist Church*, p.119
[462] Letter Blake to Allison, 28th June 2006

chaplains who were wounded, gassed or suffered 'battle shock' as Post Traumatic Shock was then known. The feeling of identification with those who suffered the horror of war was well expressed by Fisher in the dedication of his book *Khaki Vignettes* He wrote:

To my comrades
The Brotherhood of the living,
The sacred fellowship of the dead.[463]

This also expresses succinctly the new association between the churches and the State that was created through the furnace of this war. As W. P. Rhodes C.F.(U.B.) reflected about his work after the major Somme offensive of 1916.

> The rush is over at length, and now we must hurry to the aid of those who lie in helpless agony in those shell-smashed trenches. But though we are working till perspiration pours down our faces, the waiting to some seems eternally long. Mingled with their cries come the heart-breaking calls of those who lie broken in death-strewn No Man's Land. The sights around create a brain-storm, and one feels the need to cry out some word and find relief. 'Oh, God, why don't You step in!' sobs out the heart, Ah! It would not do even to try to tell the night-mare of horror that met the eye on that summer morning. But if England knew, it would say, 'Never again, never again: some other way will have to be found.[464]

Yet out of this desperate scepticism came enthusiastic support for new initiatives such as the 'League of Nations.' The religious media was happy to report on this, reprinting substantial extracts from the sermon preached before the beginning of this assembly. Ernest A. Payne, a future Secretary of the U.B. stated: "Many still believed that the conflict of 1914-18 had been 'a war to end war' and that the League of Nations would secure perpetual peace"[465] At this time there was also a growing anxiety concerning the activities of Adolf Hitler, who had come to power in 1933, when the persecution of the Jews had begun. The British Evangelical Alliance Council had already expressed its disgust in a resolution on the 27th April 1932 which recognised how the Jews were suffering "at the hands of those who profess and represent the Christian faith"[466] in Germany. The *Baptist Times* also joined in condemning the Nazi regime as early as 1933. In this article the writer reflects that

---

[463] Fisher, *Khaki Vignettes*, p.1
[464] Smith, *Stories from the Front*, p.35
[465] Payne, *Short Story*. p.194
[466] Ibid, p.197

> The accounts of the ill-treatment of Jews in Germany came as a shock to the world... The persecution of the Jews is a recurrent blot upon the pages of history, but Germany has stepped back hundreds of years and tarnished a glorious past. Nothing but evil can come of the Hitlerite policy in stirring the passions of the people against the Jewish race. The consequences may be and ought to be very severe. It is no use talking of brotherhood while Jews are dragged through the streets, their property destroyed, their bodies maltreated, even when their lives are spared. The responsible authorities in Germany should put on sackcloth and ashes, and lament and seek forgiveness. We hope that the entire Christian Church will unite in protest against these outrages.[467]

In his book *My Struggle* Hitler described his destructive philosophy and expressed the idea that: "Perhaps the pacifist-humane idea is quite a good one in cases where the man at the top has first thoroughly conquered and subdued the world to the extent of making himself sole master of it."[468] The war seemed inevitable and it was declared by Britain and its Empire once again in September 1939.

[467] Keith W. Clements, 'A Question of Freedom? British Baptists and the German Church Struggle.' *Baptists in the Twentieth Century*, London: The Baptist Historical Society 1983, p.97
[468] Adolf Hitler, *My Struggle*, London: Hurst and Blackett Ltd, 1938, p.120

Chapter Six

Conclusion

The 'United Navy and Army Board' was established on the 14th January 1915 with four constituent denominations, the Baptist and Congregational Union and the Primitive and United Methodists. Other denominations would later be administered by the U.B. as it grew in numerical strength and confidence. This organization, formed for the promotion of Free Church interests, began life as the 'United conference' (U.C.) and as such had already provided chaplains for commissioning. The first two U.B. chaplains were commissioned and sent to France on the 9th October 1914 and traditionally is the date given for the beginning of the U.B.

During the Great War (1914-1918) the U.B became a formidable organization under the charismatic and practical leadership of J. H. Shakespeare. He had an intense vision of what the U.B. could be and what it could achieve. Shakespeare saw it as proto-type of a 'Free Church of England' that could bring the Free Churches together ecumenically and together stand on equal terms with the national church without asking for its favor. Shakespeare also saw an opportunity to enhance the prestige of the Free Church by gaining formal recognition within the nation's military. The clearest indication of this acceptance was the commissioning of U.B. chaplains. This led the U.B. to take particular interest in the correct denominational attestation of its members serving in the military. This interest was generated because chaplaincy provision was supplied on a denominational quota basis and if the denominational numbers were inaccurate, often because they were being forcibly put down as Church of England, then this would limit the number of U.B. chaplains that could serve in the forces. If the practice of Free Church members being wrongly attested continued then this would also open the Free Churches up to the accusation of being unsupportive of the war for 'Christian Civilization' and again their prestige, and their hard won role in post war Britain, would have been seriously threatened. It is therefore no small achievement that the members of the U.B. remained supportive of the rights of Conscientious Objectors, even if they lacked sympathy with their views, and seriously opposed their ill treatment. This illustrated the U.B.'s moral courage when upholding Free Church principles in a national climate that tended to despise those who would not fight or support those that were.

However the U.B.'s main concern was mission and that is how these divergent denominations were able to work effectively together. They had an evangelical understanding of their role and held common objectives. The evangelical climate in the A.Ch.D at the time, under Bishop Taylor Smith, Chaplain General also suited their particular and often unique approach to ministry within the forces. The 1905 Welsh revival had influenced many UB chaplains and through the frequent use of the 'volunteer service' they were free to present the good news of Jesus Christ in a revivalist fashion and they rejoiced to see many giving their lives to Christ. These 'revival fires' were severely dampened by the attrition of the war and flu pandemic that swiftly followed in its wake. In spite of this U.B. chaplains were satisfied that their gospel ministry had prevented many from entering a Christ-less eternity.

The freedom the U.B. chaplains had was total. The 'sending church,' through the U.B. decided on promotions and even on occasion tasked directly a serving chaplain to follow up an issue of concern. As with the other recognized denominations they had their own Principal Chaplain. This gave them 'top cover' and encouraged them to remain true to their own Free Church heritage. The U.B. Minutes frequently illustrate U.B. chaplains raising concerns and frustrations with Shakespeare rather than going to the A.Ch.D. leadership. This independent thinking was reinforced by the fact that the serving chaplains held temporary commissions and remained the pastorally for their churches and remained answerable to their 'Deacon's Court.' And yet they had discovered much about the other denominations, including the Roman Catholics that allowed them to work closely with them while serving within the military. Their thinking on the sacrament or ordinance of Holy Communion had developed and communion was celebrated, by U.B. chaplains at every opportunity often using the 'Common Cup.' The U.B had introduced great positive change within the British nation's life and in the process had been changed.

Bibliography

Primary Sources

Books

Bickersteth	*The Bickersteth Diaries 1914-1918,* London: Pen & Sword, 1995
Birmingham, George A.	*A Padre in France,* London: Hodder & Stoughton, 1918
Blackburn, Harry W.	*This also happened on the Western Front,* London: Hodder and Stoughton, 1932
Clayton, P. B.	*Plain Tales from Flanders*, London: Longman's, Green & Co, 1929
Creighton, O.	*With the Twentyninth Division in Gallipoli,* London: Longmans, Green and Co, 1916
Day, Henry, C.	*A Cavalry Chaplain*, London: Heath Cranton Ltd, 1922
Dunn, J. C.	*The War the Infantry Knew 1914 - 1919,* London: Abacus, 1994
Ewing, William,	*From Gallipoli to Baghdad*, London: Hodder & Stoughton, 1917
Feilding, Rowland	*War Letters to a Wife,* Kent: Spellmount, 2001
Fisher, Phil J.	*Khaki Vignettes,* London: Joseph Johnson, 1917
Fisher, Phil J.	*Figures and Phases of the War 1916-1919*, London: Odhams Ltd, c1920
Forbes, E. A.	*Vermelles: Notes on the Western Front by a Chaplain,* Edinburgh: The Scottish Chronicle Press, 1918

Kennedy, E. J. *With the Immortal Eleventh Division,* London: Hodder & Stoughton, 1916

Studdert-Kennedy *The Unutterable Beauty The Collected Poems of G. A. Studdert-Kennedy,* Cornwall: Diggory Press, 2006

Lloyd George, David *War Memoirs of David Lloyd George Vols 1& 2,* London Odhams Press Limited, 1934, 1936.

Ed: McLaren, Stuart J. *Somewhere in Flanders. A Norfolk Padre in the Great War. The war letters of The Revd Samuel Fredrick Leighton Green MC,* Norfolk: The Lasts Press, 2005

Ed: Munson, James *Echoes of the Great War. The Diary of the Reverend Andrew Clark 1914-1919,* Oxford: Oxford University Press, 1985

O'Rahilly, Alfred *The Padre of Trench Street. The Jesuit Priest Who Gave His Life for His Men & His God at Ypres* West Sussex: Diggory Press, 2005

O' Rorke *In the Hands of the Enemy,* London: Longman's, Green and Co, 1915

Perkins, A. M. *Between Battles,* London: T. Fisher & Unwin, 1918

Ross, D. M. *A Scottish Minister and Soldier,* London: Hodder and Stoughton, 1917

Scott, Fredrick G. *The Great War As I Saw It,* Ontario: C.E.F. Books, 1999

Sellers, William E. *With Our Fighting Men,* London: R.T.S., 1916

Sellers, William E. *With Our Heroes in Khaki,* London: R.T.S., 1917

Ed: Smith, Henry *Stories from the Front by United Methodist Chaplains,* London: Henry Hooks, 1917

Spurr, F. C. — *Some Chaplains in Khaki An Account of the Work of Chaplains of the United Board,* London: Kingsgate, 1916

Tattersall, T. N. — *The Man who refused a Kingdom. A Study in Temptation,* Glasgow: Thomson & Cowan Publishers, c1920

Thornton, Guy — *With the ANZACS in Cairo,* London: H. R. Allenson Ltd, 1916

White, John — *With the Cameronians (Scottish Rifles) in France,* Glasgow: John Smith & Son, 1917

Articles

From: Baptist Times and Freeman 1914-1918

From: Christian World 1914-1918

From: Scottish Baptist Magazine 1914-1918

Charteris, W. C. — 'A Baptist Chaplain Mistaken for a Spy or a Funeral at the Dead of Night', *R.A.Ch.D. Journal,* December 1977 Vol. 24, No.128.

Petrick, H. — 'The Tasks of the Baptist Denomination in Germany', *The Baptist Quarterly,* Vol.4, No.4, September 1928

Pollock, James — 'West United Free Church. Religious Aspects of YMCA work in Flanders', *Stirling Journal and Advertiser,* December 13th 1917

Memoranda: — *The United Navy and Army Board for the Four Denominations.* c1916

Baptist Union / Committee Meeting Reports and Other Manuscripts

United Conference Minutes 1914, held at Regent's Park College, Oxford

United Board Minutes 1915 - 1919, held at Regent's Park College, Oxford

Baptist Union of Great Britain and Ireland Minute Book 1914-1919, held at Regent's Park College, Oxford

Baptist Union of Scotland Minute Book 1915-1926, held in the Scottish Baptist History Archive, Glasgow

Baptist Union of Scotland Minute Book 1926-1931, held in the Scottish Baptist History Archive, Glasgow

Baptist Union of Scotland Year Books, held in the Scottish Baptist History Archive, Glasgow

Baptist Union of Wales Year Books, held in the Scottish Baptist History Archive, Glasgow

Baptist Union of Great Britain and Ireland Year Books, held in the Scottish Baptist History Archive, Glasgow

Congregational Year Books, held at the Congregational Library, London

Ayr Baptist Church Deacons Minutes 3rd December 1914 - 7th April 1926

Royal Army Chaplains Department Journals 1931-2000

HMSO Officers Died in the Great War 1914 - 1919 His Majesty's Stationary Office London 1919

Ministry of War Personnel: Records

Ash, John C.F. WO339/126157
Ashpool, A. C. C.F. WO374/2484
Billings, A. J. C.F. WO374/6395
Bray, A. E. O.B.E. C.F./R.N. WO339/45198
Brown, Henry Martin C.F._WO374/9800

Bury, H. C.F. WO339/137942
Caldwell, Matthew C.F. WO374/11788
Cambell, George C.F. WO374/71087
Clifford, Ernest O. C.F. WO339/71087
Cowie, Peter B. W. C.F. WO374/16008
Dawson, J. T. C.F. WO 339/46277
Dight, Edward C.F. WO374/19746
Dunbar, J. W. C.F. WO374/21101
Edwards, Thomas C.F. O WO374/22217
Fairfax, Frank, C.F. WO339/138021
Fisher, Paul, C.F. WO374/24443
Fraser, Donald D.S.O. C.F. WO329/126671
Forbes, E. A. C.F. WO339/66220
Grierson, J. C.F. WO374/29328
Heading, W. H. C.F. WO374/32239
Hayward, E. E. C.F. WO374/32163
Hayward, T. C.F. WO374/32183
Hardy, J.H. C.F. WO339/138706
Hart, T. W. C.F. WO374/31579
Harte, G. W. C.F. WO372/31592
Harvey, J. Lamb C.F. WO374/31713
Hogan, William C.F. WO374/33996
Hogbin, F. A. W. C.F. WO374/34013
Horton, Paul Frederick LCpl. S/351992
Howell, Thomas C.F. WO339/132548
Humphrey, F. C.F. WO339/59966
James, Henry C.F. WO374/37002
Johnson, T. M. C.F. WO374/37771
Jollans, William M.C. C.F. WO334/37947
Jones, A. E. C.F. WO374/38016
Jones, Hugh C.F. WO374/38243
Jones, Ishmael C.F. WO374/38287
Jones, William Evans C.F. WO339/110561
Kendall, George, C.F. WO374/113278
King, William Vaughan C.F. WO 339/108369
MacBeath, John C.F. WO374/43566
Martin, E. A. C.F. WO374/46385
Maishman H. C.F. WO374/45057
Minnear, Garth Ewart M.C. C.F. WO339/130171
Morris, S. G. C.F. WO374/49010
Motley, H. C.F. WO374/49298

Patten, John A. M.C. C.F. WO339/100847
Patterson, D. T. C.F. WO374/52656
Pay, J. D. C.F. WO374/52805
Pennell, Thomas J. C.F. WO374/53356
Price, F. M. C.F. WO374/55182
Proctor, T. H. C.F. WO339/74999
Rendall, J. C. C.F. WO374/56924
Rice, G. M. C.F. WO374/57135
Snelgrove, R. M. C.F. WO339/65642
Simmons, M. B. C.F. WO374/62426
Tattersall, T. N. D.S.O. C.F. WO339/129939
Wheeler, F.H. D.S.O. C.F. WO339/116243
Veryard, Albert T. C.F. WO339/114165

Denominational Personnel: Records

Acroyd, George William C.F. The Congregational Library, London
Burns, Joseph Dobson C.F. The Congregational Library, London
Edwards, Evan C.F. The Congregational Library, London
Hardy, James Henry C.F. The Congregational Library, London
Howell, Thomas B.A. C.F. The Congregational Library, London
Patten, John Alexander M.C. M.A. C.F. The Congregational Library, London
Rees, Silas B.A. B.D. C.F. The Congregational Library, London
Smissen, George M.B.E. M.C. & Bar C.F. The Congregational Library, London
Stanley, George M.C. C.F. The Congregational Library, London
Wakey, Frank J. M.C. C.F. Spurgeon's Baptist College Files, London
Wheeler, Frank Harris A.T.S. D.S.O. C.F. The Congregational Library, London
Williams, Joseph Edger R.N. The Congregational Library, London
Robert, Peris Williams C.F. The Congregational Library, London

R.A.Ch.D. Records

Fraser, Donald
Jones, William Edger
Tomkins, William Henry
Patterson, David Tait
Veryard, Albert Thomas
Wood, Harold William

The London Gazette Supplement

First Supplement of Friday, the 20th of October, 1916.
Third Supplement of Friday, the 29th of December, 1916.
Sixth Supplement of Friday, the 1st of June, 1917.
Third Supplement of Friday, the 21st of December, 1917.
Second Supplement of Friday, the 1st of February, 1918.
Fourth Supplement of Tuesday, the 5th of February, 1918.
Sixth Supplement of Tuesday, the 5th of March, 1918.
Sixth Supplement of Friday, 22nd of March, 1918.
Fourth Supplement of Tuesday, the 2nd of July, 1918.
Second Supplement of Friday, the 23rd of August, 1918.
Fifth Supplement of Friday, the 30th of May, 1919.
Twelfth Supplement of Friday, the 30th of May, 1919.
Sixth Supplement of Tuesday, the 8th of July 1919.

Correspondence

Letters Re: Charteris held in my personal files

To N. Allison from Mark Offord 13th March 2000
To N. Allison from John Tucker 3rd March 2005

Letters; Re: Speirs held in my personal files

To N. Allison from B. Speirs 7th November 1996
To N. Allison from B. Speirs 18th March 1997
To N. Allison from B. Speirs 6th April 1997
To N. Allison from B. Speirs 13th November 1997
To N. Allison from B. Speirs 22nd April 1998

Letters; Re: Tattersall held in my personal files

To N. Allison from Mark Offord 13th March 2000

Letters; Re: Onslow-Carleton held in my personal files

To N. Allison from ? 10th July 2006

Website

Williams, Peris — *Diary of the Rev Peris Williams, Army Chaplain, 1914-1916* The Website for Welsh Cultural History Visited 06/04/2005; 16/05/2006

Secondary Sources

Books

Armitage, Michael — *The Royal Air Force. An Illustrated History*, London: Cassell Publishers Ltd, 1993

Balfour, Ian L. S. — *Revival in Rose Street: Charlotte Baptist Chapel, Edinburgh 1808-2008*, Edinburgh: Rutherford House, 2007

Bassett, T. M. — *The Welsh Baptists*, Swansea: Ilston House, 1977

Bebbington, D. W. — *The Non-Conformist Conscience Chapel and Politics 1870-1914,* London: Allen & Unwin, 1982

Bebbington, D. W. — *Evangelicalism in Modern Britain. A History from the 1730's to the 1980's*, London: Unwin Hyman, 1989

Ed: Bergen, Doris L. — *The Sword of the Lord Military Chaplains from the First to the Twenty-First Century*, Indiana: University of Notre Dame, 2004

Brown, Callum G. — *The Death of Christian Britain Understanding Secularization 1800-2000*, London: Routledge, 2001

Brown, Kenneth D. — *A Social History of the Nonconformist Ministry in England and Wales 1800-1930*, Oxford: Clarendon Press, 1988

Ed. Cecil, Hugh & Liddle, Peter H. — *Facing Armageddon. The First World War Experience*, Barnsley: Pen & Sword, 2003

Ed: Clements, K. W. — *Baptists in the Twentieth Century*, London: Baptist Historical Society, 1983

Ed: Cooper & Gregory	*Signs, Wonders, Miracles Representations of Divine Power in the Life of the Church*, Suffolk: Boydell & Brewer, 2005
Ed: Cooper, Kate & Gregory, Jeremy	*Retribution, Repentance, and Reconciliation*, Suffolk: Boydell, 2004
Dobbie, Ian	*Sovereign Service SASRA 1838-1988*, Cheshire: S.A.S.R.A., 1988
Ellis, Christopher	*Gathering A Theology and Spirituality of Worship in Free Church Tradition*, London: S.C.M., 2004
Ellsworth-Jones, W	*We Will Not Fight: The Untold Story of World War One's Conscientious Objectors*, London: Aurum Press Ltd, 2007
Fisher, John S.	*Impelled by Faith A Short History of the Baptists in Scotland*, Stirling: Scottish Baptist History Project, 1996
Grundy, Michael	*A Fiery Glow in the Darkness, Woodbine Willie Padre & Poet*, Bath: Osborne Heritage, 1997
Herspring, Dale R.	*Soldiers, Commissars, and Chaplains Civil - Military Relations since Cromwell*, Maryland: Rowman & Littlefield, 2001
Hitler, Adolf	*My Struggle*, London: Hurst & Blackett Ltd, 1938
Holmes, Richard	*The Western Front*, London: B.B.C., 1999
Horne, Jonathan	*The Best of the Good Fellows The Diaries and Memoirs of the Rev. Charles Edmund Doudney M.A. C.F. (1871-1915)*, Jonathan Horne Publications, 1995
Johnstone, Tom James	*The Cross on the Sword Catholic Chaplains in* Hagerty, *the Front,* London: Geoffrey Chapman, 1996

Johnson, Dale A. *The Changing Shape of English Nonconformity 1825-1925*, Oxford: Oxford Press, 1999

Jones, Tudor Jones *Congregationalism in England 1662-1962*, London: Independent Press Ltd, 1962

Jones, Tudor Jones *Faith and the Crises of a Nation Wales 1890-1914*, Cardiff: University of Wales Press, 2004

Keegan, John *The Face of Battle. A Study of Agincourt, Waterloo and the Somme*, London: Pimlico, 1976

Kendall, H. B. *The Origin and History of the Primitive Methodist Church* 2 Vols, London: Edwin Dalton, 1905

Laurence, Anne *Parliamentary Army Chaplains 1642-1651*, Woodbridge, Suffolk: Boydell & Brewer, 1990

Langston, E.L. *Bishop Taylor Smith A Biography of the Right Reverend John Taylor Smith K.C.B. C.V.O. D.D. Bishop of Sierra Leone, 1897-1901*, London: Marshall, Morgan & Scott Ltd, 1939

Louden, Stephen H. *Chaplains in Conflict The Role of Army Chaplains since 1914*, London: Avon Books, 1996

McNaughton, William D *The Scottish Congregational Ministry: 1794-1993*, Glasgow: The Congregational Union of Scotland, 1993

Middlebrook, Martin *The First Day of the Somme 1 July 1916*, Barnsley: Pen & Sword, 1971

Moynihan, Michael *God on our side. The British Padre in World War 1*, London: Secker & Warburg, 1983

Ed Moynihan, Michael *People at War 1914-1918*, Devon: David & Charles: Newton Abbot, 1973

Morgan, D. Densil *The Span of the Cross. Christian Religion and Society in Wales 1914-2000*, Cardiff: University of Wales, 1999

Murray, Derek B. — *Scottish Baptist College Centenary History 1894-1994*, Glasgow: Scottish Baptist College, 1994

Neill, Ivan — *Far from Tipperary. An Army Chaplain's Adventure of Faith*, Uckfield: Ivan D. Neill, 2000

Nietzsche, Fredrich — *Twilight of the Idols / The Anti-Christ*, London: Penguin, 1968

Payne, E. A. — *The Baptist Union A Short History*, London: Carey Kingsgate Press Ltd, 1958

Pitt, Barrie — *1918 The Last Act*, Barnsley: Pen & Sword, 2003

Pope & Wheal — *Dictionary of the First World War*, Barnsley: Pen & Sword, 1995

Purcell, William — *Woodbine Willie a study of Geoffrey Studdert Kennedy*, London & Oxford: Mowbray, 1962

Raw, David — *"It's Only Me" A Life of the Rev Theodore Bayley Hardy*, Carlisle: Frank Peters Publishing Ltd, 1988

Randall, Ian M. — *Evangelical Experiences A Study in the Spirituality of English Evangelicalism 1918 - 1939*, Carlisle: Paternoster, 1999

Randall, Ian M. — *Spirituality and Social Change The Contribution of F B Meyer (1847-1929)*, Carlisle: Paternoster Press, 2003

Randall, Ian M. — *The English Baptists of the 20th Century*, Didcot: The Baptist Historical Society, 2005

Ed. Robbins, Keith — *Protestant Evangelicalism: Britain, Ireland, Germany and America, c1750 - c1950*, Oxford: Blackwell,1990

Ed: Robinson & Hair — *Reflections on the Battlefield from Infantryman to chaplain 1914-1919: Robert J. Rider*, Liverpool: Liverpool University Press, 2001

Rosman, Doreen — *The Evolution of the English Churches 1500-2000*, Cambridge: Cambridge University Press, 2003

Sell, Alan P. F. & A. R. Cross — *Protestant Nonconformity in the Twentieth*, Carlisle: . Paternoster Press, 2003

Shepherd, Peter — *The Making of a Modern Denomination. John Howard Shakespeare and the English Baptists 1898-1924*, Cumbria: Paternoster Press, 2001

Ed: Smith, Swallow Henry & Trefry — *The Story of the United Methodist Church*, London: Hooks, c.1932

Smyth, John — *In This Sign Conquer*, London: A. R. Mowbray & Co Ltd, 1968

Snape, Michael — *God and the British Soldier Religion and the British Army in the First and Second World Wars*, Abingdon: Routledge, 2005

Snape, Michael — *The Redcoat and Religion: The Forgotten History of the British Soldier from the Age of Marlborough to the Eve of the First World War*, London: Routledge, 2005

Snape, Michael — *The Royal Army Chaplains' Department: Clergy Under Fire*, Suffolk: Boydell Press, 2008

Ed. Strachan, Hew — *The Oxford History of the First World War*, Oxford: Oxford University Press, 1998

Talbot, Brian R. — *Standing on the Rock A History of Stirling Baptist Church 1805-2005*, Stirling: Stirling Baptist Church, 2005

Taylor, Gordon — *The Sea Chaplains. A history of the Chaplains of The Royal Navy*, Oxford: Oxford Illustrated Press, 1978

Thomson, Ronald W. — *Ministering to the Forces: The Story of the Baptist and Congregational Chaplains and the Work of the United Navy, Army and Air Forces 1914-1964* Brighton: The Baptist Union of Great Britain and Congregational Union of England and Wales, 1964

Townsend, W.J. *A New History of Methodism*, 2 Vols, London: Workman, H. B. & Hodder & Stoughton 1909 Eayrs, G.

Travers, Tim *The Killing Ground. The British Army, the Western Front & the Emergence of Modern War 1900 - 1918*, Barnsley: Pen & Sword, 1987

Watts, Michael R *The Dissenters Volume II. The Expansion of Evangelical Non-Conformity*, Oxford: Clarendon Press, 1993

Whitley, Maurice *J. Taylor Smith K.C.B D.D. Everybody's Bishop*, London: The Lutterworth Press, 1938

Wolffe, John *God and Greater Britain Religion and National Life in Britain and Ireland 1843-1945*, London: Routledge, 1994

Wilkinson, Alan *The Church of England and the First World War*, London: S.P.C.K., 1978

Wilkinson, Alan *Dissent or Conform? War, Peace and the English Churches 1900-1945*, London: S.C.M., 1986

Winter, Jay & *1914 - 1918 The Great War and the Shaping of the 20th Century*, London: B.B.C. Baggett, Blaine, 1996

Unpublished Theses

Allison, Neil E. 'Baptist Military Chaplaincy 1914-1918,' M.Phil. University of Wales, 2006

Coulter, David 'The Church of Scotland Army Chaplains of World War Two,' Ph.D. University of Edinburgh, 1997

Coleman, Jim 'Models of RAF Chaplaincy, Ph.D University of Nottingham, 1995

Robinson, Alan Charles 'The Role of British Army Chaplains during World War Two,' Ph.D. University of Liverpool, December 1999.

Thompson, J. H. 'The Free Church Army Chaplain 1830-1930,' Ph.D. University of Sheffield, October 1990

Articles

Allison, Neil E. 'Shakespeare's Man at the Front: The Rev'd W. C. Charteris OBE MC, *Baptist Quarterly,* Vol. 41, No.4, October 2005

Allison, Neil E. 'T. N. Tattersall DSO: His War Experience and Medals,' *The RAChD Journal,* Vol.45, 2006

Allison, Neil E. 'Baptist Chaplains Revivalism at the Front (1914-1918)', *Baptist Quarterly*, Vol. 42, October 2007

Annesley, E. 'As Others See Us', *R.A.Ch.D Journal* Vol. 27, No.1, July 1982

Aubrey, M. E. 'John Howard Shakespeare, 1857 - 1928', *Baptist Quarterly,* Vol.17, No. 3, July 1957

Bebbington, D. W. 'Baptist Members of Parliament, 1847-1914', *Baptist Quarterly,* Vol. 29, No. 2, April 1981

Blackburn, H.W. & Sykes 'The Status and Work of a Chaplain', *R.A.Ch.D. Journal* Vol.1, No.1, January 1922

Clements, K. W. 'Baptists and the Outbreak of the First World War, *Baptist Quarterly,* Vol.26, No. 2, April 1975

Drury, W. 'The Initial Organization of the Army Chaplains' Department in the British Expeditionary Force, 1914-1915', *R.A.Ch.D. Journal* Vol.1, No.1, January 1922

Easey, Margaret A. 'Outline History of the Royal Army Chaplains' Department,' Unpublished article May 1998

Farrer, A. J. D. 'The Present Position of Church and Dissent,' *Baptist Quarterly,* Vol.2, No.5, January 1925

Gleig, G. R. — 'A Chaplain-General's Nunc Dimittis,' *R.A.Ch.D. Journal* Vol.3, No.29, January 1930

Gibson, A. H. — 'In Memorium: Harry Blackburn 1914-1919', *R.A.Ch.D. Journal* Vol.18, No.94, September 1963

Griffith, Gwilym O. — 'Absolute Pacifism', *Baptist Quarterly,* Vol.9, No.8, October 1939

Hawken, Cooper G. — 'How the Army can help Foreign Missions of the United Board Churches', *R.A.Ch.D. Journal* Vol.2, No. 8, October 1923

Henry, S. D. — 'Scottish Baptists and the First World War', *Baptist Quarterly,* Vol.31, No.2, April 1985

Howson, Peter J. — 'Deaths among Army Chaplains 1914 - 1920', *Journal of the Society for Army Chaplains*, Vol.83, No.333, Spring 2005

Hughes, W. B. — 'Religious Work Amongst Soldiers. August 1914 to September 1915', *The Journal of the R.A.Ch.D.* Vol.6, No.47, January 1939

Hutchings, H. W. — 'A Baptism of Fire', *R.A.Ch.D. Journal* Vol.13, No.74, September 1958

Payne, E. A. — 'Illusion and Failure? Efforts for Peace Before World War 1,' *Baptist Quarterly,* Vol.28, No.7, July 1980

Pollard, F. Ward — 'The Rev T N Tattersall DSO; An Appreciation, *The Scottish Baptist Magazine,* Vol.47.2, March 1921

Randall, Ian M. — 'The Role of Conscientious Objectors British Evangelicals and the First World War,' *Anabaptism Today*, February 1996

Rusling, G. W. — 'The Nonconformist Conscience', *Baptist Quarterly,* Vol.22, No.3, July 1967

Shakespeare, Geoffrey 'John Howard Shakespeare', *Baptist Quarterly,* Vol.17, No.2, April 1957

Sparkes, Douglas C. 'Percy Holden Illingworth and the Last Liberal Government', *Baptist Quarterly,* Vol.39, No.7, July 2002

Statton, Basil 'Chaplains of India The Story of the Indian Ecclesiastical Establishment', *R.A.Ch.D. Journal* Vol.24, No.127, July 1977

Thorold, E. H. 'The Right Reverend Bishop John Taylor Smith KCB CVO DD', *R.A.Ch.D. Journal*, Vol.6, No.46, July 1938

Tobias, M. 'A Soldiers Religion', *R.A.Ch.D. Journal*, Vol.4, No.37, January 1934

Townsend, Michael 'John Howard Shakespeare: Prophet of Ecumenism', *Baptist Quarterly,* Vol.37, No.6, April 1998

Trench, G. F. 'Mervyn George Haigh, Temporary Chaplain to the Forces, 1916-19', *R.A.Ch.D. Journal*, Vol.17, No.90, September 1962

White, Harry 'Ministering to the Forces', *The Baptist Times*, 4 June 1964

Wickramasinghe, W. G. 'Christianity and Peace', *Baptist Quarterly,* Vol.13, No.5, January 1950

Wilkinson, Alan 'The Paradoxical Chaplain', *R.A.Ch.D. Journal*, Vol.40, No.1, January 2001

Commonwealth War Graves Commission

Heading, William Henry	Cambridge UK Died 21st November 1918
Horton, Paul Fredrick	West-Vlaaderen Belgium D of W 28th September 1917
Jones, William Evans	Aisne France KIA 8th Oct 1918
Veryard, A. T.	Pas de Calais France KIA 28th June 1917

Appendix One

Baptist Chaplains

Name	Degree	Position	Decoration	Notes
Ashpool, A C		CF		
Benskin, F G		CF		
Billings, A J		CF		
Bray, Albert Edward		CF/RN	OBE	CF1915-2 RN 20-24 Died of Wounds received 1915, in 1924
Caldwell, M		CF		
Campbell, G C F		CF		
Charteris, William Cramb		CF	OBE MC MID x 3	
Clements, P A		CF		
Cleal, W J		CF		
Clifford, E O	BA	CF		
Cook, H	MA	CF		
Cowie P B W	MA	CF		
Crole, J S		CF		
Dawson, J T		CF		
Dight, E H		CF		
Doel, Horace G		CF		
Dunbar, J W		CF		
Edgerton, Arthur G		CF		
Edwards, J R		CF		
Edwards, T O		CF		Sec. C/F
Fraser, Donald		CF	DSO	KIA France 02.06.1918. Buried Couin New British Cemetery in Pas-de-Calais
Freeman, J D	MA	CF		
George, Tom P		CF		
Gower, Harry F		CF		
Gratton H J		CF		
Griffin, R C		CF		

Griffith, Gwilym O		CF		
Hainswood, T B		CF		
Hart, Thomas W		CF	MC	
Harte, George W		CF		
Harvey, J L		CF		
Hayward, Edward E	MA	CF		
Hayward, Thomas		CF		
Heading, W H		CF		Died of Influenza 21.11.18.Buried Chatteris General Cemetery
Hiley, David J		CF		
Hoare, Henry G	BA	CF		
Hodgson, J		CF		
Hogan, William		CF		
Hogbin, F A		CF		
Holme, Ralph		CF		
Hughes, Levi G		CF	MBE	
Humphrey, Fredrick J H		CF	DSO MID x 4	
Jackman, J H		CF		
James, Henry	BA BD	CF		
Johnson, Thomas M		CF		
Johnson, T J		CF		
Jones, A E O		CF		
Jones, Hugh		CF		
Jones, Ishmael		CF		
Jones, J		CF		
Jones, R Emrys		CF		
Jones, Sydney J		CF/RAF	MC	CF 15-18 RAF 18-29
Jones, Thomas		CF		
Jones, W E		CF		KIA 08.10.18. Buried in Prospect Hill Cemetery Gouy Aisae
Kemp, Forster G		CF		
Ketley, Ernest W		CF		
King, William Vaughan BA		CF		
Laslett, George H R		CF		
Lonsdale, William		CF		
MacBeath, E John	MA	CF		

MacIntosh, Donald		CF	
Maishman, Howard		CF	
Mander, H C		CF	
Martin, Edward A		CF	
Morgan, A R		CF	MC
Morgan, D J		CF	
Morris, S G		CF	
Morse, D G		CF	
Motley, H		CF	
Owen, W G		CF	
Patterson, David T		CF	
Pay, Joseph D		CF	
Page, Walter S	BA BD	CF	OBE
Pearce, J H	BA	CF	
Pennell, Thomas J		CF	
Piggot, E F		CF	
Price, F M		CF	
Procter, T H	MA PhD	CF	
Puttock, H		CF	
Rendall, James C	MA	CF	
Rhys, Thomas T	BA BD	CF	
Rice, George M		CF	
Roberts, Boaz W		CF	
Roberts, David M		CF	
Roberts, Fredrick W		CF	
Rose, Charles S		CF	
Seeley, J		CF	
Skeens, A W		CF	
Simmons, Morley B		CF	
Skeens, Arthur W		CF	
Smith, Leonard G E		CF	
Snelgrove, R M		CF	
Stearn, C H	BA BD	CF	
Sutton, E F		CF	
Tattersall, T N		CF	DSO MiDx3
Thomas, Charles		CF	
Thomas, H G		CF	
Thompson, Cecil H		CF	
Thompson, Herbert H		CF	
Thomson, Malcolm M BA BD		CF	

Tomkins, W H Buried in		CF	KIA 28.09.18. Cagincourt British Cemetery Pas-de-Calais
Veryard, A T		CF	KIA28.06.17. Buried in Roclincourt Military Cemetery
Walker, David		CF	
Walker, J R		CF	
Walkey, Frank John		CF	MC OBE
Warwick, T		CF	
Watson, E L		CF	
Weeks W R		CF	
White, A J		CF	
Wilkinson, Samuel H		CF	
Wood, C		CF	
Wood, H W		CF	Died of Wounds 01.11.18. Buried in Terlincthun British Cemetery Pas-de-Calais
Yorwerth, William M		CF/RN	CF(16-20) RN(24-39)

Congregationalist Chaplains

Ackroyd, George William		CF
Adams, J		CF
Allen, S W		CF
Ballard, F H		CF
Banton, A E		CF
Bartlett, R		CF
Berry, R W		CF
Bevan, J		CF
Bevan, T J		CF
Bignell, P E		CF
Bohn, J C A		CF
Bonsey, A W	BA	CF
Booth, T C		CF

Bunce, H		CF	
Burns, Joseph Dobson		CF	Died of Wounds 07.06.18 Buried at Ebblinghem Military Cemetery, France
Buxton, F L		CF	
Catterall, J E		CF	
Carleton, O W M		CF	
Caunce, W G		CF	
Clarke, J W	MA	CF	
Clayton, J L L		CF	
Coates, W J	BD	CF	
Cooper, J P		CF	
Crookall, E	MA	CF	
Daniels, W E		CF	
Davies, D E	BA	CF	
Davies, R W		CF	
Davies, T L		CF	
Docker, F E	MA BD	CF	
Dyson, J		CF	
Eaton, I H		CF	
Edwards, Evan		CF	Died of pneumonia in Tidworth 30.11.18 Buried Anfield Cemetery, Liverpool
Edwards, J	BA	CF	
Elliott, N		CF	
Evans, J	BA	CF	
Farrington, A		CF	
Foulston, W W	BA BD	CF	
Fox, A E		CF	
Gamble, H J	BA	CF	
Giffin, J W		CF	
Gruffydd, E J		CF	
Haley, L	BA	CF	
Hall, C W		CF	
Hall, E		CF	
Hardy, James Henry		CF	KIA 05.05.18 Nine Elms British Cemetery,

Belgium

Hartley, J		CF	
Herbert, D C		CF	
Holland, E H		CF	
Hosking, J	BA	CF	
Howell, Thomas	BA	CF	KIA 01.12.17 Villers-Plouich, France
Howells, J A		CF	
Hughes, R W		CF	
Inglis, J W	BA	CF	
Isaac, J J		CF	
Jenkins, E	MA	CF	
Johnson, R W		CF	
Jones, E	MA BD	CF	
Jones, E		CF	
Jones, R		CF	
Joseph, T F		CF	
Knowles, H		CF	
Lansdown, A P		CF	
Laundy, S R		CF	
Lawson, A C	MA	CF	
Lawson, E J	MA	CF	
Lewis, R		CF	
Matheson, A E	BA BD	CF	
Mathias, E		CF	
Mathews, G	MA BLitt	CF	
Maxwell, A R		CF	
McClelland, H S	BA BD	CF	
Mead, A	BA	CF	
Milnes, J H	MA	CF	
Moffatt, A U		CF	
Murphy, T C	MA	CF	
Newell, H W	BA	CF	
Omerod, J C	MA	CF	
Onslow-Carleton, William		CF	KIA 11.1918. Lost at sea, off the coast of Ireland
Pace, W H		CF	
Parry, E		CF	
Parry, H		CF	

Primitive Methodist Chaplains

Barber, B A	CF	
Bellew, W E	CF	
Bishell, C T	CF	
Callin, W R	CF	
Delafield, S G	CF	
East, T S	CF	
Emmitt, E S	CF	MC
Firth, John	CF/RAF	MC MID
Fisher, P J	CF	
Gilbert, J E	CF	
Gray, A G	CF	
Grayson, J W	CF	
Grierson, J	CF	
Hancox, T A	CF	
Harper, T	CF	MC
Heward, T B	CF	
Horne, E de J	CF	
Kendall, G	CF	
Leggate, H	CF	MC
Lowe, A	CF	
Mowforth, S E	CF	
Musson, W J	CF	
Parlow, J J	CF	
Parnaby, W N	CF	
Sands, T	CF	
Scott, G T	CF	
Smith, E W	CF	
Spedding, R K	CF	
Standing, George	CF	MC DSO
Swinnerton, W	CF	
Tubb, W J	CF	
Wearmouth, R F	CF	
Woodward, H H	CF	

United Methodist Chaplains

Allen, H D		CF		
Ash, John		CF		KIA 07.09.17 Vlamertinghe New Military Cemetery, Belgium
Ashton, F W		CF		Died of Pneumonia in Sheffield 04.11.18
Bolitho, H		CF		
Bowyer, A E		CF		
Chambers, F H		CF	OBE	
Checklin, G T		CF		
Clarke, T E		CF		
Davey, J P		CF	CMG	
Dewdney, W		CF		
Fairfax, F		CF		
Field, W		CF	OBE MID Croix de Guerre	
Gibbon, J		CF		
Hinchcliffe, H		CF		
Hulse, A H		CF		
Jeffries, W H		CF	MC	
Jollans, W		CF	MC	
Langley, J E		CF		
Lockettt, A C		CF		
Minnear, G E		CF	MC MID	
Raine, Foster		CF		Died: self inflicted 09.09.18
Reeves, A F		CF	MC	
Rhodes, W P		CF		
Strong, R	MA Blitt	CF		
Wallett, J		CF		
Walters, G F		CF		
Welsher, E J		CF	MC	
Wooldridge, R H		CF	MC MID	

Appendix Two: Inter War Period

Baptist Chaplains

Alexander, William		CF		
Bellin, Wynford		CF		
Bray, Albert Edward		RN	OBE	CF(1915-) RN(1920-24)
Clyde, William Alexander		CF		
Cowie, Peter B W	MA	CF		
Collinge, Norman		RAF		
Hughes, L G		CF	MBE	
Jeffray, George A		CF		
Jones, Sydney J		CF/RAF	MC	CF (1915-18) RAF(1918-29)
Lund, Richard	BA	CF		
Marsh, Walter Robert	BD	RAF	KHC	
Miller, G F	BA BD	CF		POW 1941
Potts, A J PC		RAF	CBE	1936-
Schofield, John N	MA BD	CF		Resigned 1935
Shears, Frank W		CF		31-34
Thomas, David M		CF		31-34
Yorwerth, W M		RN		CF (1916-20) RN (24-39)

Congregationalist Chaplains

Appleyard, J R	RAF	
Evans, D D L	CF	CBE
Haig, A	RN	
Clynes, W A	RAF	
Spearing, A E	RN	

Primitive Methodist Chaplains

Firth, J	RAF	MC
Roebuck, O	RN	

United Methodist Chaplains

Barker, A G	CF	MC
Bennett, E E	CF	
Bowyer, A E	CF	
Penry, J P	CF	CMG
Gibbon, J	CF	
Jollons, W	CF	MC
Langley, J E	CF	
Leonard, J E	CF	
Mansfield, R E	CF	
May, F J	CF	
Reeves, A F	CF	MC
Rhodes, W P	CF	
Sandercock, S	CF	
Spencer, F	CF	
Wallett, J	CF	
Welsher, E J	CF	MC
Winter, E S	CF	
Wooldridge, R H	CF	MC